For Phyllis Taylor –
Whom I met on the ocean,
but who taught me about the land.

The Anthologies:

THE ANTHOLOGIES

HINTERLAND

TAHIR SHAH

THE ANTHOLOGIES

HINTERLAND

TAHIR SHAH

SECRETUM MUNDI PUBLISHING
MMXX

Secretum Mundi Publishing Ltd
PO Box 5299
Bath BA1 0WS
United Kingdom

www.secretum-mundi.com
info@secretum-mundi.com

First published by Secretum Mundi Publishing Ltd, 2020

THE ANTHOLOGIES: HINTERLAND

© TAHIR SHAH

Tahir Shah asserts the right to be identified as the Author of the Work
in accordance with the Copyright, Designs and Patents Act 1988.
A CIP catalogue record for this title is available from the British Library.

Visit the author's website at: www.tahirshah.com

ISBN 978-1-912383-44-3

Contents

Introduction

WHEN I WAS a child, I read a story about a fearless explorer named Jonjo who had crisscrossed every corner of the globe in search of treasure.

Jonjo was fearful of nothing, and there were no lengths to which he would not go to track down the treasure at hand.

One day, someone asked Jonjo to reveal his secret, for he'd managed to find treasure on a scale unmatched by anyone else – dead or alive.

Jonjo thought long and hard, then he said:

'The secret of finding treasure is looking inland.'

Taking the book from home to school and from school to home, I told everyone I met about Jonjo's secret:

'You have to look inland,' I would tell them, 'otherwise you won't find treasure.'

On receiving the information, some people reacted in gratitude. But most of them laughed at me. They said I was an idiot for spouting nonsense, and that my young age was no excuse at all.

Luckily for me, I never listened to those who pushed me down or mocked Jonjo and his wisdom.

Instead, I found myself turning the fragment of truth over in my head. While other children dreamt of Lego, I dreamt of a world inland – a realm set far from the shore.

One day at Langton House, where I grew up, a visiting elderly gentleman asked me about my interests. I told him that the only thing I was really interested in was searching for treasure inland rather than at the coast.

'You mean in the hinterland?' he asked.

'*Hinterland*?'

'The hinterland... A place that's far inland.'

I've heard of famous scientists or painters being touched by a seminal moment in their childhood. That was it for me. My ears sucked the word in – *Hinterland* – my mind's voice playing it over and over like a mantra.

Weeks passed, and the book with Jonjo's story was put on a shelf too high for me to reach, probably in the hope that I would move on to a fresh obsession. But I knew the tale so well I no longer actually needed it in my hand and, in any case, the way I told it to myself had improved on the real thing.

I would tell anyone and everyone who'd listen that I was going to the HINTERLAND! The way I said it, and thought about it, the word was written in capitals with an exclamation at the end.

HINTERLAND! – the realm of Jonjo's treasure...

I regarded the hinterland as a country blessed with all kinds of riches.

Go inland and you encounter subtle differences from the world beyond the shore. Point yourself in the direction of the interior and you find yourself on a trajectory that can only end in wonder – whether it be a cultural treasure, or one fashioned from gold, fit for Jonjo himself.

Tahir Shah

The Field of Reeds

ANCIENT EGYPTIAN FOLKLORE describes an Elysian realm known as Aaru, the so-called 'Field of Reeds', to which the souls of mortals journey after death.

Although ever curious when it comes to folklore, I didn't know much about the treasury of myths dating back to Ancient Egypt. That is, not until the friend of a friend pointed me in the direction of a small village lost in the desert between Luxor and the Red Sea.

The details provided were sketchy: a foreigner who didn't speak Arabic was living with the locals, and was behaving in a very strange way.

I remember thinking it wasn't worth investigating, and being told by my informant that I'd 'thank the Heavens' if I went.

Having been holed up writing a novel in the Winter Palace Hotel in Luxor for as long as I could remember, I was ready for a break.

So, although dubious, I agreed to go take a look.

Spend any time in Luxor and you can't help but acquire hangers-on. Within an hour of arriving at the railway station, I had a money-changer, a barber, a fixer, and a guide. Egypt's unwritten rule is that hangers-on give the traveller preferential treatment in return for availing of their services rather than those of the competition.

I'd been a regular visitor to Luxor, and a guest at the gloriously faded jewel of the Winter Palace, since my teens. Taken to Upper Egypt first by my parents, I found the city perched at the edge of the Nile to be a pleasure dome of exotic adventure.

Random attacks, revolutions, and the general instability of the Middle East had caused fickle khaki-clad tourists to go elsewhere for their Oriental fix.

Although shameful of me to admit it, part of the draw of Luxor was the lack of tourists. My travels tend to zigzag between destinations low on security and high on the unusual. As far as I'm concerned, there's nowhere quite as perfect to lie low and write than in the faded grandeur of a cut-price palace hotel.

That's how I found myself in a spacious suite,

the floor hardwood parquet, with a vintage fan whirring round on the ceiling above.

Over the weeks I stayed at the Winter Palace, I engaged more and more hangers-on – dozens of them.

On the scale of retainers none could compare with Mustapha.

A goliath of a man, a life-long passion for mutton kebabs had got the better of him. As he reminded me frequently, he was the finest taxi driver in all Upper Egypt.

Whenever I'd step out from the Winter Palace's revolving door and stroll down one of the curled twin flights of stairs, Mustapha would screech to a halt on the street below. The tyres of his battered old Peugeot 504 would be smoking, the exhaust belching out clouds of poisoned gas.

Quite how Mustapha knew I would be exiting the hotel when I did was one of Luxor's great mysteries. I put it down to a kind of magical telepathy between us.

On the morning of the journey into the desert, I casually mentioned the plan to the bellboy on the way down to breakfast. By the time I was ready to leave, I found a line of the hotel's staff poised to the right of the door.

The manager wished me good fortune and reminded me to trust no one.

The concierge provided me with a map, on which danger zones had been marked in red felt-tip pen.

The maître d'hôtel bowed, and clapped his hands twice.

A pair of staff with small feet shuffled out, lugging an oversized hamper forwards at double speed.

'A little light lunch, monsieur.'

Before I could reach the revolving door, the concierge scrutinized the directions provided by my informant. Checking them against the map he'd given me, he scowled, his expression disapproving.

'Please forget this unwise journey,' he urged. 'Go out to the pool and lie in the shade.'

Thanking him, and his colleagues, I made my way through the revolving door, emerging in the dazzling morning light.

A minute later I was down on the street,

where Mustapha's decrepit Peugeot was waiting for me.

Clambering in, I handed over the directions. Mustapha studied them intently.

'Will this car make it?' I asked.

As though I were enquiring whether a warhorse was capable of enduring a battle, the veteran driver tugged a rag from his wrist, mopped his brow, and gave a double thumbs up.

'Very good,' he affirmed. '*No broblem*!'

Three hours passed, in which the Peugeot shrieked and groaned along metalled roads pocked with holes, then down telescoping tracks. Either side of the oily smog-trail belching out behind us, the desert spanned out from horizon to horizon.

Mustapha put on a tape of rousing love songs by the vintage Egyptian heartthrob, Hafez.

From time to time he would glide to a halt, mop his brow, and glance wearily at the instructions.

Whenever I offered the map, he'd wave it away, as though swiping a fly buzzing around his head.

Like all Egyptian taxi drivers, Mustapha had

no faith at all in cartography. The only thing he trusted was information provided by word of mouth.

That meant screeching to a stop as soon as anyone was spotted herding sheep near the track. More often than not it was a child of six or seven.

Having exchanged elaborate greetings, shared water, conversed, laughed, asked, listened, commiserated, and thanked God half a dozen times, we would press on a little further... until the next underage shepherd came into view through the Peugeot's cracked windscreen.

The sun arced its way up into an empty sky.

We passed a large, dented, sand-swept sign. It featured a hand-drawn skull and crossbones, against what appeared to be an illustration of an explosion.

'The danger zone!' I roared, jabbing a finger to the map.

'*No broblem!*' Mustapha shot back.

'Are you sure?!'

The taxi driver nodded, then shook his head.

'Very good!' he muttered. 'Very very good.'

Another hour came and went before the

Peugeot overheated. While waiting for the engine to cool, I unbuckled the hamper and scattered the Winter Palace's feast over a picnic blanket on the rock-strewn ground.

Eyes lighting up at spying food, Mustapha chomped his way through three plates of sandwiches, half a leg of lamb, and a cherry trifle – its dish designed to be cooled by an in-built ice basin. Long since melted, the ice had transmuted through desert alchemy into boiling water. Discovering it, Mustapha let out a cry of joy, and brewed a flask of tea.

Eventually, the engine cooled and we pushed forwards, faltering and jerking on for another hour and a half.

As I drew breath to give the order for retreat, Mustapha's index finger motioned at the horizon.

Drowned in mirage up ahead lay a cluster of homes.

'D'you think that's it?' I asked.

Mustapha cackled and whooped:

'Very good! Very good!'

Veering off the track, the Peugeot 504 navigated a zigzagging course between boulders and ditches, until it reached the clutch of frail stone houses.

Villagers streamed out as we appeared.

A minute or two after that, Mustapha and I were staggering through the searing heat from the vehicle to the shade, calling greetings as we went.

I wasn't sure whether to reveal right away the reason for our expedition, or to let things naturally progress. My travels had taught me when possible to favour the second option.

Having reached the villagers, we shook hands, thanked God, and ran through the catalogue of pleasantries preceding the rituals of desert hospitality. We were coaxed into one of the stone houses to drink tea, and to rest.

In the Western world unexpected visitors may well be regarded with suspicion, the opposite is true in the vast expanse of desert in which we found ourselves. Another difference that often struck me was the balance between chatter and silence.

In the Occident, a newcomer might expect to be bombarded with questions and drawn into protracted conversations. In Arab lands, silence is more revered than even the most enlightened exchange of words.

So, we sat there, drinking tea, with no enquiry as to why we had come or where we were going. Poised beside me, Mustapha broke the silence by thanking God.

Resorting to the magical telepathy between us, I pushed him to enquire about the foreigner. Before any such question could be voiced, the villagers spoke:

'He arrived a month ago,' said the first.

'With little luggage, no shoes and dressed in rags,' added a second.

'He doesn't speak our language,' explained a third.

'Where is he now?'

'Under the ground,' the first villager said.

'He's *dead*?!'

'No... not dead...'

'Then what is he doing underground?'

'Sleeping.'

'*Sleeping*?'

'He sleeps a lot of the time.'

'Why?'

The villagers conferred, argued, agreed and, in unison, replied:

'We don't know.'

'Can I meet him?' I asked.

'If God wills it.'

The villagers led me out into the blazing light.

As we crossed the patch of empty ground, circumventing a low hill, I tried to imagine what they must have thought of the mysterious foreigner arriving on foot.

On the far side of the hill, one of the villagers strode over to a crude stone doorframe set at an angle against the gradient. Pulling away a sheet of corrugated iron, he led the way down a set of steps carved into the rock.

At once the insufferable heat was replaced by extreme refrigeration, ice-cold shadows, and a faint scent of rotting meat. Following the others down, I readied myself for the unexpected.

But that certainly didn't prepare me for what came next.

The stairs led down to an antechamber. As I descended into the darkness, I tried to work out if the structure was a remnant of the Ancient Egyptian era. In some ways it was like the tombs I had visited in the Valleys of the Kings and Queens. But there were no hieroglyphs. Instead of the plaster favoured by the ancients, it appeared as though the walls were rendered in cement.

My eyes calibrating to the lack of light, I paced through the antechamber, and down a long corridor – a conduit into the main chamber.

The room was illuminated by a dozen shafts of blinding light. Somehow channelled from ground level, they took my breath away. I remember puzzling at being so impressed. After all, a few minutes before there had been abundant light. But only now that it was limited, did I notice it at all.

Mustapha's silhouette strode through to the centre of the chamber which, I suppose, must have measured about a hundred foot square. As I drew closer, and as the others moved out of the way, I caught first sight of what I was later to describe as the 'altar'.

Crafted from a series of stone blocks, it reached chest height.

Outstretched upon it, was the body of a blonde man.

Bare feet together, both arms were crossed over the torso in mummy stance. His eyes were closed. Had I not been told he was alive, I might have assumed the reverse.

We stood there, watching.

Succumbing to the talc-like dust, I sneezed, automatically excusing myself.

The foreigner opened one eye, and then the other.

Lifting his head, he scanned the chamber.

'Someone speak English?'

'Sorry,' I said. 'It's terribly dusty down here.'

Sitting up, the man appeared intensely sleepy, as though he'd been hibernating all winter.

'What are you doing here?' he muttered, an accent to his English.

'Just passing by,' I replied, adding, 'what about you?'

The foreigner jumped off the altar, completed the ritual of shaking hands, and said:

'I'll tell you over a cup of tea.'

So we left the chamber with its glorious shafts

of light, and retraced the route back into the realm awash with illumination.

'I am Dieter... Dieter from Switzerland,' the blonde foreigner said, leading me to a low stone shack at the edge of the hamlet. 'They've given me this to use.'

'What about the cavern down there?' I asked, looking over my shoulder. 'What's that all about?'

'First tea, then I will explain.'

So Dieter cooked up a pot of tea. Then he clicked his neck, his shoulders, his finger joints, and his toes, inhaled and exhaled, and regarded me through ocean-blue eyes.

'Wish I could tell you I'm a crackpot,' he said. 'I'm sure that's what you think of me. After all, being out here as I am, lying on a slab ten metres under the desert... I can imagine it would look odd.'

Dieter folded the mop of hair from the left side of his head to the right. As he did so, I wondered how old he was. I guessed about thirty-five.

'I've seen stranger things,' I countered.

Studiously, Dieter the Swiss narrowed his eyes and let out half a laugh.

'I should like to hear about them.'

'I'm more interested in hearing how you ended up in the desert,' I replied.

'Through a journey that began with a hunch.'

Dieter explained how, as an anthropologist with an interest in Pharaonic Egypt, he was obsessed with their notion of Aaru, the so-called 'Field of Reeds' to which the souls of mortals venture in the afterlife.

As Mustapha the taxi driver dozed out in the shade, Dieter the Swiss described the route thus far.

A journey from the town of Aarau, in the canton of Aargau, to the remote desert hamlet in which we'd met.

'"Aaru" sounded rather like "Aarau",' he said at the end of the explanation, 'which is how I came to be interested in Ancient Egypt as a child.'

'Why don't you just study the hieroglyphs like everyone else?'

Dieter rubbed a thumb to either eye, and sighed out of the corner of his mouth.

'Because I want to understand it in a different way.'

'Is that why you arrived here barefoot and without any backup?'

'It's part of it.'

I asked how he came to hear of the chamber.

'It was left by a Swiss field unit who were doing work here back in the 'sixties,' he said. 'My PhD supervisor had been involved. He told me all about it, and even gave me the key. I didn't want to freak out the villagers, so I turned up in the most discreet way possible. To my delight it was still here. The only problem's been trying to explain what I'm doing.'

'They think you're a nutcase,' I said.

'Yeah, I know.'

'They're wondering how long you're going to stay.'

Dieter the Swiss coaxed the mop of blonde hair from the right side of his head back to the left.

'Wish I knew the answer to that myself.'

I accepted a second cup of tea, my mind struggling to frame questions.

'Don't quite get how lying down there in the

dark is going to magically transport you to the Field of Reeds,' I said.

Again, Dieter sighed through the corner of his mouth.

'I've spent the last ten years with anthropologists, psychologists, students of philosophy, and a never-ending cast of serious men and women. Each one of them tackles the research in exactly the same way. Once in a while one of them branches out and poses what appears to be a radical new approach. Yet, even at best, they never stray from the path mapped out by those who came before them.'

'So you're blazing an entirely new trail?'

'Yes, in some ways I am.'

We sat in silence for a few minutes, listening to the stray breeze tearing over the desert. In different circumstances I might have given voice to my many questions. Somehow, though, it didn't seem like the right time.

But there was something I needed to know.

When the breeze had died down, and our ears were both tuned in to Mustapha snoring outside once again, I asked Dieter how he'd come to think like he did.

The answer that came was not the one I had been expecting.

'When I was a kid,' he said, 'at bedtime my parents used to read me stories about a very funny man. He wore a big, white turban on his head, had a long, flowing beard, and rode a donkey backwards. Sometimes he was the king, and at other times he was a beggar. But no matter whether he was rich or poor, he always saw the world in a fresh "back-to-front" way.' Dieter paused, as though wishing to make a point. 'His name was Nasrudin,' he said.

A shiver coursed down my spine.

'Amazing,' I whispered.

The Swiss anthropologist from Aarau rummaged in a daypack and pulled out a hardback book. The covers were desperately scuffed, as if they'd withstood a sandstorm.

'This is it,' he said, passing it to me.

Opening it to the title page, I read:

'*The Exploits of the Incomparable Mulla Nasrudin*, by Idries Shah.'

From *Travels With Nasrudin*

In the Empty Quarter

A CARAVAN OF dromedaries snaked its way northward across the border from Oman.

On the back of each camel was a pair of wooden crates stencilled with Hannibal's monogram and with the word 'ARABIA'. Stretching out between the animals and the horizon lay a vast emptiness of honey-yellow sand.

From time to time towering dunes came and went, rising like mountains into the cobalt sky. Against such an awe-inspiring panorama, the slim cortège of beasts and men was nothing at all.

At the head an Arab named Khalil al-Khalil led a magnificent camel – her back laden with crates like all the rest. A great brute of a man, Khalil claimed to have crossed the Rub' al-Khali, the fearful Empty Quarter, twice before – the first time as a gunrunner, the second while spying for the Omani Secret Service.

Little more than a brigand, he was a liar, and frequently a thief. In reality, Khalil had never set foot anywhere near the Empty Quarter. Even now, he had only been coaxed to join the current expedition with the enticement of cold, hard cash.

Thirty feet behind him, leading another dromedary, was a second man in Bedouin dress; most of his face was shielded by a turban. The only hint he was an outsider was the patch of skin around the eyes. Roasted red and raw, Will's face was so blistered that he had taken to sleeping with a damp towel wrapped over his face at night.

Behind him, some way after the camels and their crates, was Emma and, behind her, Chaudhury. Like Will, they were both dressed as Bedouins – coarse camel hair robes, turbans drenched black with sweat.

Khalil had promised a fabulous oasis another few miles to the north. He said they would camp there, refresh the animals, refill the water skins, and continue at dawn. Will and the others hoped this time their guide would come good on his promises.

Until then he had shown no skill at all in the ways of desert survival. The fact was that anyone who had really been in the Empty Quarter avoided it like the plague. They would not have returned for any sum of money. The hostile nature of the terrain made it the perfect place to hide an object for eternity.

Trudging, one foot after the next, the group moved listlessly in the direction of the distant horizon, like gassed soldiers retreating from the Front. In the two weeks since setting out from Salalah on the Omani coast, their bodies had been scorched, and ravaged day and night by fleas.

Technically speaking, they had crossed into Saudi Arabia, in what was just about the most desolate region on Earth. Even the Bedouin steered well clear of the Empty Quarter if they could help it. As far as they were concerned, it was Hell on Earth.

The sun's heat reached its crescendo and, as it did so, Khalil thrust an arm above his head. Pointing at a far-off speck close to the horizon, he claimed it to be their salvation – the oasis.

Three hours later, the caravan reached a clump of desiccated date palms. Hidden among them were a jumble of parched animal bones and sun-baked water skins. There was dried mud too, cracked and brittle, but not a single drop of water.

Realizing there was no hope, Khalil fell on the ground and thrashed his arms about as he wept. He begged forgiveness, beseeching God to provide sustenance in the form of a miracle.

Then, conjuring his last strength, he got up and ran impetuously into the desert. Will called to him to stop, but Khalil didn't listen. Shrinking against a grim backdrop, he vanished into the dunes.

'We're better off without him,' said Emma caustically.

'Means we can finally break into the gear,' added Will. He trudged over to where a little pool of water had once stood, scooped up a handful of the dried mud and crumbled it between his fingers.

'Chaudhury, please bring box number five,' he said.

The manservant staggered down the line of dromedaries and urged the last one to sit. As it groaned and glowered, he untied the bindings and off-loaded a wooden crate.

Will jemmied off the side, revealing an early

form of dehumidifying machine, designed by Hannibal Fogg back in 1912. Powered by electrolysis, it had an in-built hygrometer for measuring relative humidity. Sucking moisture from the air, it collected the precious liquid in a cylindrical reservoir.

The Empty Quarter was so dry that the device strained for an hour before it had gathered sufficient water to alleviate their thirst.

'The camels need to drink, too,' said Will, 'but this thing's never going to satisfy them.'

'How far d'you think it is to the Notification Quadrant?' asked Emma.

'Can't be more than another eighteen miles. Then about the same again before we reach the grid reference. If we push hard we should make it by dusk.'

Clambering up, they set off, with Will at the front. For an hour they made headway, the dromedaries moving in a slow trot despite their burdens and their thirst.

Just as they thought they were making good progress, the sky went sienna-brown, the sun extinguished by a searing wind sweeping in from the west.

'Sandstorm!' screamed Emma.

'Get down!'

Throwing themselves onto the ground, they heaved the camels to kneel, nuzzling into their flea-infested underbellies, as Khalil had shown them to do.

A tornado ripped through.

It was so abrasive that it stripped the packing crates of their paint, tearing away the bindings.

The camels groaned as if the world were about to end. Forcing himself into the folds of flesh, his back in line with the animal's shank, Will struggled to transport his mind far away.

He thought of the ordered corridors at Penshaw, Willis, Smink & Co in London, where his journey had begun. Focusing hard, he pictured the details exactly – the long oil portraits of elderly men in legal robes, the chesterfield in the waiting room, an Oriental rug laid over scuffed floorboards.

As he played the scene over and over, the sand-wind ripped past and disappeared. Half-wondering if he had gone deaf, Will unfurled a hand, cautiously sticking it out to his side.

The air was still, silent as a summer's day.

Lifting his head, he got out from the dune formed around him. The she-camel he had been riding had slipped into a catatonic state, a natural self-preservation system.

Will staggered over to check on Emma and Chaudhury. Like him, they were shaken, but none the worse for wear.

As he turned to calm his dromedary, Will fell backwards in shock.

All around, for as far as they could see, were bones, both human and animal – an abominable caravan of death.

From *Hannibal Fogg and the Supreme Secret of Man*

In Xanadu Did Kubla Khan

THERE COULD FEW better places to begin a *Journey Through Namibia* than at Noordoewer, on the banks of the great Orange River.

It is there that the main Namibian highway begins its run north. Wedged between the ever-shifting sands of the Namib to the west and the Kalahari's desert tundra to the east, southern Namibia is a barren but beautiful place, with some of Africa's most spectacular landscapes. Few people live there, and the plants and creatures have had to adapt to life in a harsh, dry terrain. At the first flush of rain, however, the parched landscape turns lush green.

The Orange River, which flows more than two thousand kilometres from its source in the Drakensberg Mountains of South Africa, forms Namibia's southern boundary with South Africa. It was on the southern banks of the river, in 1866, that young Erasmus Jacobs discovered a diamond. He had no idea what it was, but when he was found playing with it, diamond fever swept southern Africa. A series of finds fuelled a frenzy of greed, excitement and prospecting. The very fact that diamonds were accessible in the area was due to a natural process which happened millennia before. The Orange River – which once flowed from the interior of South Africa – cut into a Kimberlite pipe, the substance in which diamonds occur. The inherent hardness of the diamonds ensured that they survived the journey to the mouth of the Orange River, from where they were deposited along the Namibian coast.

As early as 1897, the master of a sailing vessel, Captain R Jones, sailed into the harbour at Cape Town clutching a packet of diamonds. He claimed to have picked them up on one of the many islands along the southern coast of South West Africa. Again, in 1905 and 1906, a few diamonds were found in guano which had been mined on the same offshore islands. Two years later the first diamond fields were discovered, well north of the Orange River, at a remote spot on the Atlantic fringes of the Namib called Kolmanskop.

They brought rapid change and swift development. Hamlets turned into villages, villages blossomed into towns and roads and railways were laid. When the diamond seams around Kolmanskop began to run out during the late 1920s, operations were transferred to the diamond fields at the south-eastern edge of the Namib. And prospecting moved south to the Orange River. It was thought that as diamonds had been discovered at Alexander Bay, on the Orange River's southern banks, the seam should extend to the northern banks. Theory became fact in 1928 when geologists discovered more diamond coastal terraces north of the Orange River.

Diamonds, which the ancient Greeks believed were fragments of stars that had fallen to earth, are the key to the future of this young nation. They are also the reason for the existence of the small town of Oranjemund, founded by Consolidated Diamond Mines – CDM – in 1936 at the mouth of the Orange River. The town plays an important role in the Namibian economy, having replaced Lüderitz as mining headquarters in 1943. Complete with airport, rail and bus terminals, verdant municipal parks and immaculate golf course, Oranjemund is the closest thing to Heaven in a harsh and intimidating land. It is a town of eight thousand residents without jobless or homeless people, where all medical treatment is free, and the company pumps water from the Orange River. With five thousand workers Consolidated Diamond Mines is the country's largest employer, and in recent years has established new mines at Auchas, on the banks of the Orange River, and Elizabeth Bay, just south of Lüderitz.

The *Sperrgebiet* – Forbidden Area – where diamonds lie, is a daunting barrier of black, craggy cliffs with razor-sharp ridges and spectacular rock formations, including the fifty-eight-metre natural arch of Bogenfels rock. Because of its wealth, the coast is prohibited territory to all but mine officials and workers. Dykes are built to recover diamonds below the tideline when the waters of the lagoons that form are pumped dry. Mechanical diggers remove thirty million tonnes of earth, sand and rock a year at Oranjemund alone. The diggings, spread over several hundred square kilometres, form one of the world's largest open-cast mines.

Few sights are as awesome as those of the giant excavators, the largest and most spectacular earth-movers in the world, gouging great chunks of sand and rock out of the earth down to a depth of twenty-four metres, as protective dykes hold back the ever-threatening waters of the Atlantic. When the sand and rock are pulled away, the diamond-bearing gravels are revealed and a task force of Wambo labourers, armed with simple brooms, industriously sweep forward. They search the surface for diamonds lodged in tiny cracks and crevasses – retrieving an average of six thousand carats of diamonds a day.

The scale of the operation can be perceived in the fact that for just two hundred milligrams of diamond, at least thirteen and a quarter tonnes of sand, gravel and conglomerate, have to be cleared away. These operations cost in the region of a million US dollars a day.

The biggest diamond ever recovered weighed 246 carats. Such wealth creates its own temptations, and security within the forbidden territory is a continual battle. The theft of uncut diamonds is a massive industry on its own. For every three million dollars' worth of gemstones recovered, experts estimate that another ninety per cent finds its way onto the market.

Thieves use all manner of means to smuggle out their loot. Once, X-ray machines detected a condom containing two hundred stones – while cut-away heels in shoes, hollow books and luggage handles have become commonplace discoveries to eagle-eyed security staff. Not long ago a homing pigeon was seen fluttering on a three-metre security fence; closer examination showed it was carrying a pouch so heavy with diamonds that the bird was unable to take off.

So tough is security that since 1927 no vehicle or machine has ever left the Oranjemund Diamond Mine. In fact, a vast dump – the disused equipment park – contains row upon row of lorries, trucks, bulldozers, cranes, some of the largest earth-moving equipment ever built, and acres of old tyres, all spread out over kilometres of barren landscape.

Almost a hundred per cent of the stones are of gem quality, mainly colourless or pale yellow. Namibia's 'fancy' diamonds, infrequently found, are varied in colour, often pink, and unequalled for quality.

CDM is Namibia's major taxpayer, contributing between sixty and sixty-four per cent of its profits to the national exchequer. Indeed, in 1981 it accounted for ninety-seven per cent of all tax revenue.

Production remains strictly controlled. CDM is a subsidiary of the South African De Beers conglomerate run by the Oppenheimer dynasty. When overproduction threatened prices, the family closed down most of the Namibian mines – the world's sixth-largest producer – and they continue to maintain control of the market. Although in the 1990s, when world markets were flooded by cut-price diamonds from the former Soviet Union, and illicitly mined stones from Angola, the traditional structure was close to collapse.

Consolidated Diamond Mines was also angered when an American entrepreneur was given a concession to mine diamonds between the high and low tidemarks along the forbidden coast. While they initiated legal action, the

American put a fleet of costly dredging barges to work sucking gravel from the sea bed. In the end CDM took over the operation but the potential for offshore diamonds has never been really viable.

All the way along the forbidden coast, a string of curiously named islands stretching north beyond Lüderitz underlined the strange anomaly of South Africa's continued role in independent Namibia, even as late as 1993. For if Roast Beef and Black Rock islands were part of the country's sovereignty, others such as Plum Pudding, Sinclair's, Pomona, Albatross, Possession, South Long, North Long, Halifax, Penguin, Seal, Ichaboe and Mercury islands remained marked on the map as South African territory – with no word to explain why one should be different from the other.

But there is much more to Namibia than deserts and diamonds. The dried-up course of another once mighty river of the south lingers in the mind when most other memories have faded. West of the 2,134-metre Karas Mountains, and the first stretch of highway between Noordoewer and Griinau, a winding trail leads through a bleached wasteland to one of Africa's great natural wonders. During thousands of years, the Fish River has cut a 536-metre deep chasm in the rocky, barren plains that is twenty-seven kilometres across at its widest. Twisting 160 kilometres through eroded cliff, staggering in their rugged beauty, the Fish River Canyon is one of the Earth's greatest canyons. One road runs along the edge of the canyon to a series of viewing points where sheer cliffs plunge to the river bed, which is a billion years old.

In an area often plagued by drought, the well-watered canyon, with its fish and game, was an oasis for early inhabitants. By 1981 more than forty Stone Age sites had been recorded, increasing in size where the canyon begins to widen in the south. Fish River Canyon was proclaimed a national monument in 1962, became a game reserve in 1968 and a conservation area in 1969. The reserve was expanded in 1987 to include the Huns Mountains to the west and land to the south.

The centrepiece of the canyon, which began forming about five hundred million years ago, is a ninety-kilometre nature trail, involving a four-to five-day hike. From the main lookout, the trail leads down into the canyon and Hell's Bend – a classic example of a meander which originated when the river was young. Recently a second hiking trail in the canyon, the Fish Eagle Hiking Trail, was opened. This trail in the upper part of the canyon is undertaken with a guide.

The longest river in Namibia, the Fish River, flows more than eight hundred kilometres to its confluence with the Orange River, one hundred and ten kilometres east of the Atlantic. Some kilometres south of the Gaab River, which is where the Fish Eagle Trail begins, it plunges over two waterfalls and enters the canyon. Its flow varies with the rains, usually between November and March. But it is the only Namibian river that has permanent pools outside the rainy season. In spate it becomes a raging ninety-one-metre wide torrent tearing through the gorge at up to twenty-five kilometres an hour. In 1972 it destroyed a newly built rest camp, except for the main building on the high ground.

The strata of the cliffs were initially sandstone, shale, and lava deposited almost two billion years ago. Five hundred million years later they folded over and, compressed deep in the earth's surface, heated up to more than 600°C. This caused metamorphosis, re-crystallizing the rock and changing its appearance. The dark lines which cut the canyon walls are fractures filled with lava that never reached the surface.

When the first major erosion began some 850 million years ago, it exposed the rock strata and levelled them into a vast peneplain – becoming the bed of a shallow sea that covered southern Namibia. Five hundred million years ago the crust fractured, forming a north-south valley, which was deepened two hundred million years later by Ice Age glaciers. The uplifting of the sedimentary strata in the area increased erosion caused by the river, as the glaciers began to melt, so that the gorge became deeper still. The fractures are clearly visible five kilometres along the nature trail.

Hobas, an overnight camping site, is ten kilometres from the main lookout and descent point into the canyon. After slithering down, clutching hold of the chains that slow the descent on the steeper sections, there is much to see on the valley floor. The trail leads to the palm-shaded Sulphur Springs, fifteen kilometres south. Other trees and shrubs that flourish in the valley's winter temperatures of 20-25°C include tamarisk, camel-thorn, ringwood, buffalo thorn, wild fig, ebony, euphorbia, sweet thorn and the green-hair tree.

Klipspringer – their thick, bushy coats protecting them from falls, their hooves adapted for rock climbing – haunt the canyon which is, for them, an ideal habitat, along with kudu, the nocturnal Hartmann's mountain zebra, rock dassie, ground squirrel and chacma baboon. These are stalked by leopard. Ostrich also live in the canyon where the cliffs and pools echo to the call of the purple gallinule, marsh warbler, white-backed mousebird, red-eyed bulbul, blacksmith plover, hammerkop, Egyptian goose, grey heron, Cape robin, rock kestrel, rock pigeon, chats, starling and dusky sunbird. Alternately seeking shade and heat to control their body temperature, cold-blooded reptiles, including three species of deadly African adder and the Egyptian cobra, survive among the rocks and shrubs. The canyon's perennial pools sustain good numbers of barbel and yellow-fish, providing ideal sport for the angler.

The impressive Four Finger Rock dominates the halfway stage of the trail and, just beyond, is the grave of a German officer killed by the Nama in 1905. From there it is a good day's walk to the hot springs of Ai-Ais, a vernacular word meaning 'Fire Water', once the home of Neolithic man. During the Nama rebellion in the first decade of this century the Germans made it their base. The 60°C waters, a mixture of fluoride, sulphate and chloride, are fed to an outdoor swimming pool and jacuzzis. Today it is a popular spa resort. From there, the Fish River winds away – through a ravaged range of forbidding and uninhabited mountains – to join the Orange River in the south.

The rest camp at Ai-Ais is open from the second Friday in March until 31st October, and hikes in the canyon are from the beginning of May until the end of September.

Gazing down into the canyon from the deep, precipitous cliffs, the words of Samuel Taylor Coleridge in his famous 1816 poem *Kubla Khan* come to mind:

In Xanadu did Kubla Khan
A stately pleasure-dome decree;
Where Alph, the sacred river, ran
Through caverns measureless to man
Down to a sunless sea...
But oh! that deep romantic chasm which
*   slanted*
Down the green hill athwart a cedarn cover!
A savage place! as holy and enchanted
As e'er beneath a waning moon was haunted
By woman wailing for her demon-lover!

Back on the main highway, Keetmanshoop forms a junction between Lüderitz and the Namib in the west, with Windhoek in the north, and the Kalahari in the east. Namibia's fourth-largest town, on the banks of the seasonal Swartmodder River, is a thriving centre founded on the site of an 1866 mission station. Linked by rail to the port of Lüderitz, Keetmanshoop became the gateway to the interior and prospered from the wealth of the southern diamond fields early this century. Wealthy prospectors could afford European luxuries, and the shops of

Keetmanshop were filled with the treasures of Paris, Berlin and London.

Others established farms or squandered their fortunes on high living and the gaming tables. The town's wide streets are lined with some superb examples of colonial architecture, notably the stone church and old post office, which is now a museum. The mission station and school, both of which are still in use today, were built by the Reverend Thomas Fenchel, who served in Keetmanshoop from 1877 to 1910.

During a flash flood in October 1890, the missionary and his family had to be rescued when their house was flooded and the church swept away. The pulpit and bible were recovered from the flood and have been preserved in the new church which the preacher built. It had room for one thousand worshippers and served all races in Keetmanshoop until 1930. Recently the church, notable for its hand-carved woodwork, was restored. The town is named after Johann Keetman, a wealthy German industrialist and chairman of the Rhenish Missionary Society.

To the east of the town, on the road to Koés, grows the eerie Quiver Tree Forest, one of Namibia's great natural curiosities. The forest's three hundred kokerboom trees, *Aloe dichotoma*, spread out some distance from each other, cover the rust-coloured slopes with a supernatural look. Like the Namib's *Welwitschia mirabilis*, the kokerboom, also known as the quiver tree, has had to adapt to its barren, inhospitable environment. Growing as high as seven metres, the fibrous trunk, spindly branches and pithy leaves develop into water containers – their slow growth and waxy surface coating help the trees withstand the arid climate. In the depth of the southern winter, during June and July, the radiant yellow flowers at the top of the plants burst into bloom, bringing the bronzed landscape to life. The San use the fibrous core of the hollowed-out branches as pincushion-like quivers for their arrows. Close by the Quiver Tree Forest is the Giant's Playground, an unusual formation of volcanic rocks, weathered over millions of years.

Spread across 130 square kilometres, the Gellap Ost Karakul Farm, also near the Quiver Tree Forest, was founded as a sheep breeding centre by Paul Albert Thorer. He imported a flock of karakul sheep, a hardy central Asian breed, into Namibia in 1907. The Namibian-bred sheepskins are regarded as the finest in the world – and include pure white karakul pelts, found nowhere else. They are taken from lambs slaughtered twenty-four hours after birth.

More than 250 kilometres east of Keetmanshoop, on the Sandheuwel Game Ranch, deep in the Kalahari Desert, more than fifty species of mammals – including the Kalahari lion – are visible from the luxury of the Kalahari Game lodge. With game drives and walks, horse-trekking and hot-air balloon safaris, the sanctuary is an oasis of delight for nature lovers.

Keetmanshoop is a turnoff for the intriguing run west through the Namib diamond field the fairy-tale town of Lüderitz. Twice a year, at Easter and in July, Namibian Railway celebrates the pioneering days of steam. A Diamond Train, hauled by a majestic Class 24 locomotive, steams the 334 kilometres from Keetmanshoop to Lüderitz. When the journey begins, a cloud of white doves are released in the bright blue Namibian sky as the train passes under a ceremonial arch at Keetmanshoop station. Aboard the train, two hundred passengers are entertained by a band, which plays a Diamond Train song composed by Crispin Clay, the bard of Lüderitz. The dining and lounge cars are decked out in the livery of the early days of the diamond rush.

About a hundred or so kilometres from Keetmanshoop on the road to Lüderitz, a spur leads thirty kilometres north to the small town of Bethanie. Its old London Missionary Society station, the first in Namibia, was founded by a German missionary, the Reverend Heinrich Schmelen. He had vowed to preach the word to the Hottentot Khoikhoi who had migrated there, but he abandoned the station in 1822 after war broke out between the Nama and the Herero. One relic of his time survives. Schmelenhaus, Schmelen's simple one-story cottage, built in 1814 – and then rebuilt after it was burnt down – is the oldest European building in Namibia. Another national monument is the house of Joseph Fredericks, the nineteenth-century Hottentot chief. It was there that the first treaty between the Germans and the Hottentots was signed.

One of nature's great surprises, Africa's only herd of desert horses roams the Namib west of Aus, a small town midway between Keetmanshoop and Lüderitz. As the chestnut steeds wander the sandflats, they seem like a mirage. The hardy creatures have adapted to life in a thirsty land. Conserving their energy, they can exist for five days without water, for the only source these creatures have is the artificial pan at Garub which is supplied from a borehole. The herd remains one of the great riddles of the Namib – no one is certain how they came to live in the hostile desert. One theory is that they are descendants of horses left behind when the German garrison abandoned their base at Aus in 1915.

From *Journey Through Namibia*

Survive!

SIMON COCHRAN LISTENED as the great clock chimed the hour.

Standing up, he motioned for Adams to do the same.

'Ladies and gentlemen,' he began, 'I am most honoured as a humble secretary to this esteemed Committee, to have the pleasure of introducing again Mr Robert Adams, and in asking that he might grace us with the continuation of his fascinating narrative.'

Thanking Cochran, Adams took in the audience. 'As I have explained,' he said, 'the surviving shipmates and I were taken as slaves towards the interior of the great Zahara. As each day dawned, we had no idea if it were to be our last. But I for one had vowed an oath to survive, that I held sacred.

'Days and nights passed in a gruesome sequence of discomfort. Each night Morales, the Spanish traitor to our faith, would approach us, jesting at our derelict condition, tempting us with clothing and morsels from our captors' table. We cursed him, called him what he was – filth vented from the sewers of Hell.

'Then one morning the camels were gathered up and the spoils from our ship rearranged upon them. The Moors whipped my shipmates and me to our feet. I shouted out to Morales, imploring him to reveal what was going on.

'"The interior is a furnace where the horses will not survive," he said. "So they will stay with us near to the coast."

'As he spoke, one of the Moors climbed down from his camel, bound my hands with a strand of leather, and tied the other end to the saddle of the beast. He shouted something in Arabic.

'"You have been traded," Morales said calmly. "You will go with the others, into the interior, and there you shall die."

'That moment was one of the most fearful I have ever had the misfortune to experience. I stood there on the sand, naked but for a strand of leather covering my manhood, my friends hauled away from me. I shouted to them, tears in my eyes, and they called back. The last word to touch my ears was Dolbie's.

'"Survive!"

'The camels moved fast across the sand. If I did not keep up with their elongated stride, they would pull me, jerking me forward like a rag doll. By the afternoon, we had entered a new territory. The sand was much dryer, and the air stripped of its moisture. I struggled for breath. All I could think was to ask myself again and again where they were taking me.

'From one horizon to the next there was a sea of sand – flat, silent, baked hard by the sun. We crossed it walking fast, as if heading to a pressing engagement.

'As soon as we had traversed the emptiness, reaching the horizon, we were rewarded with another identical vista – an eternity of sand. From time to time there might be a low thorn bush. When the Moors set eyes on such a thing they became joyful. They would rush over to it and tug at it, until the roots were exposed. One at a time they would suck them, their laughter suggesting great pleasure.

'We marched for five days. Then, in the far distance, we set eyes on what I assumed was a group of trees. Yet as we drew closer, we saw it was moving. My captors seemed pleased. They increased the pace and, by dusk, we had reached their fellow group of Moors.

'That night, there was celebration. A fire was lit and an odd-looking animal was slaughtered, its carcass roasted. I did not recognize it or its smell. And, when one of the bones was hurled in my direction, I grew yet more curious. As I huddled gnawing at the bone, I heard a voice – an English voice.

'"Are you a Christian?"

'"Yes!" said I. "Who are you?"

'"Then I am your brother," said the man. "A seaman, from Cadiz. I was wrecked three years ago and taken into slavery, as you."

'"What's your name?"

'"Juan Sanchez. And you?"

'"Robert Adams."

'I told Sanchez that I felt much misery at being separated from my companions. To which he replied that the Moors saw Christians such as ourselves as objects to be bartered with one another, that there were hundreds just like us in the great desert. Then I asked him what animal had died so that I might suck at its bones.

'"It's a desert fox," said Sanchez.

'The next morning I asked my new friend how we might reverse our sordid condition. I expected him to hang his head low. But he didn't.

'"We can escape," he said quickly, "only if we can get to Mogador on the coast of Marocco, then the Consul there will redeem us. He will pay the ransom of any man who has not forsaken the Christian faith."

'I leapt to my feet and ran as fast as my legs could carry me to the place where my master was crouched.

'"Mogador! Mogador, take us there!" I pleaded to him at the height of my lungs in English. "Help us and the Consul will make you rich!"

'The Moor got up and struck my shoulder so firmly that the ball was expelled from the socket. Then, when I howled, he licked me with his whip. The following night, after a day of terrible anguish, Sanchez ordered me to bite on the leather strap that bound my hands. As I did so, he thrust the shoulder back into place.

'We marched on for another week, a procession of camels laden with an assortment of oddities gleaned from ours and other ships. There were sails furled up in sacks, crates of hardtack, portholes threaded together on ropes, nails, hammers, and all sorts of other tools. And, on one camel – an unwieldy female – was bound the great carved figurehead of a ship, *Queen of the Waves*.

'From time to time our caravan happened upon another. The Moors would kiss each other's cheeks, praise their god, and trade ships' merchandise dug out of their packs.

'On one occasion we had been welcomed by a large gathering of Moors. My master presented his host with a pair of Bibles, the dry pages prized for tinder. The gift was well received and our host opened a chest filled to the brim with booty. Removing a spyglass and a Union flag, he offered them ceremoniously to his guest.

'As the days passed, Sanchez educated me in the art of survival upon the desert sands. He taught me to gather dew from the night air, and the skill of ruminating one's rations, like a camel, so as to gain maximum satisfaction from a meal. He taught me, too, how to drink from the flow of a camel's water without getting kicked in the face.'

From *Timbuctoo*

Gorillas in the Mist

WE WALKED OUT of Ruhengeri towards Africa's first national park, accompanied by the buzzing sound of Marcus' yo-yo running up and down its string.

Women were working in the fields, bending down and scything grass. One would sing, a scarf tied tightly about her head, as the others joined in with the chorus. A track led through meadows filled with chalky-white and yellow flowers.

The seven volcanoes of the national park suddenly came into view, protruding from the jungle like a line of camels' humps. Each was covered in a forest of trees and banana plants, which shrouded luxuriant vegetation of all kinds. One plant blended into the next. Many were bowed down under the weight of gigantic green and red fruit. We pressed on, high up into the groves of tall bamboo where the canopy was thick and became denser with each step.

A barefoot child appeared with a machete competently gripped in his hand. The machete was his stock-in-trade: he hacked through the stems, having offered to take us to where the gorillas were.

It began to rain. Some plants collected the water and stored it in their bowl-like leaves. Troops of monkeys swung from branch to branch, and birds called out warning of our arrival across the jungle.

Mountain gorillas are known for moving about one area in small groups, usually guarded by the dominant male, the silverback, who is said to have strength enough to tear a grown man limb from limb. As no one is ever quite sure where the gorillas are on any one day; it can take hours to locate them.

The boy with the machete cleaved a path just wide enough for us to ease our way through. A rhythm guided his blows, as he wielded the blade skilfully, chopping only what was necessary. We followed in single file, and behind the party the jungle closed in again, healing its wound.

The vegetation was denser than any I had seen before. One plant overlapped with another, creating an abundance of nature that seemed all but impossible for man to dominate.

Everything but ourselves was hidden as if

in camouflage and blended perfectly into the green mixture. Dressed in the colours of bright synthetic dyes, we moved with great clumsiness through the habitat: totally intrusive outsiders. We had come from the complexity of the West: where one has to study for fifteen years merely to understand something of the society that it has created. Now back in the very belly of nature, from which our forebears emerged, we were uneasy as if all around us was an alien land.

After some time we reached a small opening where the bamboo stems had been broken away. Zak and Oswaldo sat down, as the boy with the machete pointed to the end of the clearing. A family of woolly black – almost human – forms were moving about. At first they looked to me like humans dressed in gorilla suits with hidden seams.

A female clutched her baby and rocked it up and down, another picked fleas from her behind with neat precision, using the very tips of her black nails. She radiated absolute satisfaction at ridding herself of the insects.

The male silverback stamped around restlessly, as if he were waiting for the ladies to get ready to go out. Some other gorillas strolled about like a family on a spring afternoon at Brighton.

Then the male jumped to within six feet of where we stood. He peered, with a stare that seemed to pass right through us.

A glare ran across his face and his eyes were filled with tight, round drops. Could these primates have been the original people of Gondwanaland? Perhaps to them the Gond tribe was related. As I stared and wondered many things it felt as if I was being reunited with a long lost companion whom I had never really known.

Dian Fossey, author of the best-selling *Gorillas In The Mist*, had befriended these creatures. One morning in December 1985 she was found with her skull split open: supposedly the work of poachers. My travels had begun to teach me of the irresponsibility of mankind. I had seen sights of destruction created as a by-product of one form of civilization.

Ashtrays fashioned from gorillas' hands continue to be made: educated people pay for them. They will pay the price in the future. Man must realize that what he does today shapes the world that he will have to inhabit tomorrow.

The child with the machete led us back towards the edge of the forest. As he hopped through the tall bamboo, guiding us back to the main road, I wondered what would become of that place in his lifetime.

From *Beyond the Devil's Teeth*

We Are Danakil

NEXT MORNING, BEFORE the first light of dawn cut across the horizon, the salt caravan arrived.

Forty camels and ten men walked briskly into the settlement.

The camels were laden with what seemed to be large, grey slabs of stone. Like every camel on Earth, they resented being enslaved by man, but they were energetic, for their day had just begun. Their leader gave the order for the beasts to be given water and he checked the bindings of their loads. Then he came over to where we were standing.

Adugna introduced us. Kefla Mohammed was a slender man with skinny legs, calloused hands and an occasional squint. He walked with a limp, plunging his long stick into the sand as he went, like a gondolier. He must have been the same age as me, but he looked much older, his skin roughened by decades of desert sun.

When Adugna had introduced us, Kefla pressed his shoulders to mine in greeting.

'We will be friends for a thousand years,' he said.

'We wish to journey to Mekele.'

The leader stood tall, pushing himself up on his stick.

'You will walk with us and share our food,' he replied, 'for we are brothers.'

I thanked him.

'How many days' trek is it?'

Kefla took a step back.

'Far,' he said. 'It is very far.'

'Two days?'

'Perhaps.'

'More than that?'

Again he stepped back. Then he glanced at the fine sand which covered his feet.

'Perhaps.'

Two hours later our bags and our water bottles were strapped on the strongest of the she-camels, and we took our positions at the rear of the caravan. Adugna and his family stood to attention and wished us good fortune. Other villagers came to bid us farewell too, but Adugna fought them away with his stick. This was his moment. I promised to return when I had visited Mekele, when I had found the gold of Solomon.

'I have told you,' he called as we left, 'come

and stay here with me and we shall wait together for God's cloak to lift.'

Setting out on a journey of uncertain length in an unknown land is a thrilling prospect. I asked Samson if Kefla and his troop seemed trustworthy. He hugged his Bible close to his chest and hinted that they were good people but that they needed his Christian counsel. Only then, he said, would God raise his veil and restore the fortunes of the Danakil.

'Do you really believe the legend?' I asked.

Samson looked up at the sun blazing overhead.

'The Lord is wonderful and mysterious,' he said.

We trekked over parched ground, heading north-west. There was no tree cover and only a smattering of cacti and scrub. Whenever the camels spotted any vegetation, they would stop and graze. They were roped together like mountaineers and didn't seem in the least affected by the great weight of their loads.

The salt they carried had been carved from the dry bed of Lake Karum and from the salt flats around it in Afar. Long wooden poles are used to prize the blocks loose, and then the blocks are sawn into smaller pieces of a uniform size.

Kefla called us to the front and offered us some cooked meat and water from his bottle. He was eager to tell us about his life. Fortunately, like Adugna, he spoke some Amharic, and so Samson could translate.

'I have walked this route a thousand times,' he said, 'since I was a child. Before me, my father walked with the camels, as his own father did before him.'

'What of the dangers, the fear of *shiftas*?'

'These days there's no danger,' he said, 'except from scorpions and snakes. Our people used to enjoy killing foreigners but now we have come to trust them.'

Kefla glanced over at me as we walked. I knew what he was thinking. He was wondering if I'd heard of the Danakil's preoccupation with testicles.

'I have read of the proud traditions of the Danakil,' I said. 'It is sad that they have disappeared.'

'We are still proud,' he replied. 'We are Danakil. But we no longer kill every man whose face is unknown to us. That was the old way. It was a good way, but now it has passed.'

Most of the men in the party were related to Kefla, brothers or sons, nephews or cousins. They formed a strong unit, he said, each man trusting the others with his life. The salt caravan was no place for women. Kefla's wife, his third, was with the clan in the Danakil desert. They had been married the previous year, after his second wife had died in childbirth.

'What about your first wife?'

The leader thrust his stick in the sand, his gaze fixed on the ground.

'She died as well,' he said, 'of malaria.'

I changed the subject and asked about the legend of the gold.

'Ah, yes, the gold,' he said, almost as if he had anticipated my question. 'It has been turned into salt by God.'

'Do you think He will ever turn it back into gold again?'

'Perhaps,' said Kefla, 'and that would be good, as you can sell gold for a lot at Mekele. But I get angry when I hear my friends and clansmen cursing that the gold has gone. You see, God changed a useless metal into salt – and no man or camel can live without salt, but we can all live without gold.'

Nesbitt had warned of the danger of trekking with camels. He had written of the constant worry that they would catch a foot in a crack in the ground. Kefla and the others were alert for such clefts and, if there was any doubt, they would halt the caravan and probe the earth with their sticks before carrying on. Another problem was the stifling heat. I found myself drinking water incessantly. Kefla told me to be careful. Too much water, he said, was as bad as none at all. I doused a shirt in water and wrapped it around my head like a turban, and Samson did the same.

From time to time a block of salt was unstrapped from one of the camels and given to them to lick. At other times, Kefla would feel the sand with his hand. If it were too hot, the camels' feet would burn. Nothing was as important as the well-being of the camels.

Nesbitt wrote that he preferred to travel with human porters rather than with pack animals. Humans, he said, can take short cuts, negotiate precipitous slopes and cross torrents by jumping from rock to rock. More to the point, fresh porters can be hired when necessary. But then again, no man could heave blocks of salt such a great distance.

In the late afternoon, camp was pitched near a thicket of thorn trees. Samson had been keen to spread the Word of God to the Danakil, most of whom were Muslim. But now that he had a captive audience, he hadn't the strength. We sat in a heap on the ground: I was too exhausted to write my journal, and he was too tired to preach. Around us, the camels were being unloaded and watered, a fire was built and some scraps of meat were roasted. I asked Samson to find out how much further we had to go.

'Please do not make me ask that question,' he said. 'I cannot bear to hear the answer.'

So we lay there, waiting for the night, and I thought longingly of the Emperor's Jeep. I even began to think of Bahru with some affection.

Kefla told his eldest son to keep guard. He was a boy of about twelve.

'He's as wise as Suleiman,' he said, 'like his

grandfather. Many girls already want to marry him. But there is time for that.'

'You know of Suleiman?'

'Of course,' responded the leader, 'all Danakil know how he came here himself searching for ivory and gold.'

'Did he find them?'

'Yes, yes, he did. I told you, there used to be gold here. There was much gold in the time of Suleiman.'

'Did he mine it?'

Kefla stoked the fire with his stick.

'His men cut the gold from the ground in slabs,' he said. 'Then it was loaded on to ships and taken back to the land of Suleiman.'

'How did they carry the gold to the ships?'

'Suleiman's army of jinn carried it, of course.'

The camels had been fed and were now sitting, chewing the cud. The sky was lit by a crescent moon and speckled with stars, and the air was cool, chilled by a light breeze from the east. Kefla's eldest son was called Yehia. He patrolled the camp with a Lee Enfield .303. He was close to puberty, the time when his forebears would have started to prepare for their first kill. The boy's finger never left the trigger; he was clearly itching to pull back the curved sliver of steel. But he had been born too late. Deaths are still a frequent occurrence among the Danakil, but now they are put down to self-defence rather than cold-blooded murder. These days when they kill, the Danakil don't bother to rip off testicles. Although Kefla and the others didn't say so, it was quite clear that they thought killing wasn't the same if you couldn't hack off your enemy's private parts.

When he passed me, Yehia clenched his jaw and swung the rifle to his shoulder in a practised movement. As a foreigner my kind had been fair game since the beginning of time. Only now had the rules changed, and the young warrior felt cheated. I smiled at him, but his mask of rage didn't break. His uncle Abdullah invited us to sit with him on a coarse goat-hair mat. He was taller than the others, with a slim neck, and he wore a pair of bandoliers strapped across his chest. He cut a piece of dried meat from a carcass in his lap and held it to my lips.

I was about to ask how much further we had to

travel, but I knew Samson would be reluctant to translate the question. Instead I asked Abdullah about Mekele.

He frowned so hard that his brow rippled like corrugated iron.

'It is a very big city,' he said. 'Too many men, too many cars, too much noise!'

'So you don't like it?'

'Ah!' he said. 'Walk in the city and you see the worst side of man. People forget where they have come from when they reach such a place. They grow lazy and drink beer, and they waste their money. That is not the real world.'

'Then what is the real world?'

Abdullah loosened the bandoliers and then slapped his hands together and held them out like scales.

'*This* is the real world,' he said. 'Look at it! Smell it! Taste it! Listen to it!'

Kefla came over to where we were sitting and crouched on the ground. It was dark, but I could see he was tired. He said that Yehia would protect us in the night. If there was any trouble the camels would be sure to sound the alarm. They could smell a thief from a great distance.

'I hope we are left alone,' I said feebly.

Kefla smiled, and leant back on his heels.

'You may be wishing that,' he said, 'but Yehia is praying that we will be disturbed. He is ready to pull the trigger, to prove himself a man.'

All of the next day we marched, one foot ahead of the next, as the sun rose from a faint pink glimmer of light to a raging ball of fire above the desert. I found the going hard. By early afternoon it was so hot that my spit sizzled on a rock. My mind kept flashing back to the jungle. The desert was bad, but nothing could compare with the horrors of a tropical rain forest. As I staggered on, I thanked God that we were far from the jungle. We had seen no insects or reptiles, and we could walk freely, unhindered by low vines, fallen tree trunks and the press of undergrowth. Samson had never been in the jungle, so he didn't know how lucky he was. He started moaning about missing Addis Ababa, saying that his girlfriend would be longing for him, and that he had to get back to urgent commitments. His misery gave me new strength. I found myself sympathizing with Henry Stanley and his habit of throwing men in irons at the slightest whisper of dissent.

The camels were unloaded every three hours and their bindings were constantly checked. Rubbing would lead to sores. The only journey I had ever made with camels was in India's Thar Desert years before. On that trip we had actually ridden the camels, rather than walking alongside. But I'd soon come to appreciate the unique relationship between man and camel. The animals look at their masters with loathing. But the men in a caravan regard the camels with silent wonder. They would never admit it, but you can see that they value the beasts as highly as their closest friends. This was never more apparent than when one of Kefla's camels went lame.

It was the late afternoon of the third day and Kefla was leading the caravan through a series of low, barren hills. We were all exhausted. The camels were about to rest and be watered. We had grown used to being blinded by light so dazzling that it scorched our retinal nerves and made our eyes stream with tears. Somehow, the

Danakil coped with the brightness and remained alert to the camels' every move. They needed to: a single misplaced step could spell disaster. Then, suddenly, one of the smaller she-camels plunged to the ground and let out a truly terrible bellow of pain.

Without wasting a second, Kefla took a knife from beneath his shawl and sliced away the straps which held the slabs of salt. The animal thrashed in agony and her bellows turned to a high-pitched shriek. With the others struggling to keep her still, Kefla made a quick inspection. It was obvious that her right foreleg had shattered. Then the caravan's leader picked up his knife and pressed it against the camel's neck. '*Bismillah ar-rahman ar-rahim*, In the name of Allah, the Beneficent, the Merciful,' he cried.

With a whack of the blade, the animal's jugular was severed. Blood gushed out of the wound as the camel kicked in a last frenzied gallop, her eyes rolling, her mouth wide open. A few moments later she was dead.

Kefla stood over the carcass, his knife still wet with blood. There were tears in his eyes. He covered his face with his hand and then wiped it with the edge of his shawl. I was not surprised that a Danakil was weeping. His friend was dead. While the other men unloaded the rest of the camels, Kefla walked away into the distance to be alone.

From *In Search of King Solomon's Mines*

Thief with a Conscience

ON THE JOURNEY back to Meknès the next day, we passed rows of stalls at the side of the road, manned by an army of teenage boys.

They sold avocados and chameleons, bouquets of roses, and red ceramic pots.

There were no villages or houses for miles around. I wondered how the boys got there or why they had selected such a remote setting for their trade. We had not planned to stop, but when I saw the chameleons being held up cruelly by their tails, I ordered Kamal to hit the breaks. I sent him to buy up their entire lizard stock – twenty chameleons in a range of sizes. They cost me five hundred *dirhams*, about thirty pounds.

It was daylight robbery.

Five miles after the stalls, the road was empty again, lined with eucalyptus trees and scrub. The sunlight was so bright that Kamal shielded his eyes with his hand as he drove. He said he couldn't remember a brighter afternoon. The road curved to the left, then the right, and evened as it rolled on towards the north. For

the first time in a long while we had a good view ahead.

A man was waiting in the shadow of a fir tree before the horizon. He was bent over with age, his body shrouded in a hooded *jellaba*. I saw him first.

'Let's give him a ride,' I said, 'and we can set the lizards free at the same time.'

'Those people are nothing but trouble,' said Kamal.

'What about charity? Please stop. You must stop,' I said.

Kamal eased down on the brake and we slid to a slow, awkward stop. The man limped over with his knapsack. I called out to him in greeting and told him to climb aboard. He grunted thanks. While he staggered over, we got out to liberate the chameleons. A second later, we heard the sound of the engine starting. I swivelled round to see the Jeep driving off. It is a moment I will not forget. We dropped the lizards and ran up the road, shouting insults.

It was no use. The car was long gone.

'Bastard,' I said.

'May Allah steer him into a tall tree,' Kamal quipped.

'Don't say that. I don't want the car damaged.'

'You're not going to get it back,' said Kamal. 'By nightfall it'll be cut up in Meknès and sold for scrap.'

We sat at the side of the road in disbelief, waiting for something to happen. He didn't say it, but I sensed Kamal blaming me for buying the lizards. They had led to our downfall.

'Poor lizards. Poor old man,' I said defensively.

'Damn the lizards, screw the old man. He wasn't even old. He was just pretending to be old,' said Kamal. 'He was a thief.'

After fifteen minutes of waiting, we heard a car approaching from the direction of Meknès. It was the first vehicle we had seen. The road was so straight that we caught sight of it long before it reached us. The car was moving very fast, sunlight reflecting off the roof. I screened my eyes with my hands.

'It looks like the Jeep.'

Kamal peered out to the distance. 'It is the Jeep,' he said.

'Is he coming back for the shirts off our backs?'

'Let me handle this,' said Kamal.

He picked up a sharp-edged stone and ran towards the car as the thief skidded to a halt.

'Don't hit him!'

'Of course I'm going to hit him!'

The thief opened the driver's door a moment before Kamal reached him with the stone. He was shouting something in Arabic. It sounded as if he was begging for mercy. Kamal's expression was one of passionate anger. I had seen his wrath before. He was quite capable of killing if he wanted to. The thief shouted again, clambered out and lay spread-eagled on the ground. I didn't understand what was happening. He was pleading, repeating the same words again and again.

'What's he saying?'

Kamal didn't answer. He tossed away the stone, visibly moved. His fury melted away.

'What's he saying? Why did he come back?'

The man begged for mercy.

'*Allahu akbar*! God is great!' said Kamal.

'What?'

'I can't believe it.'

'What?!'

'He says that he brought the car back to us because...'

'Because?'

'Because if he did not, no one would ever stop to help an old man again.'

From *The Caliph's House*

Tale of Hatim Tai

THE CAR WAS buried in a sand drift. It looked as if it had been stuck there for weeks.

'When did you last use it?'

'Two days ago.'

'So much sand in two days?'

'It's the wind,' said Fouad. He opened the back, grabbed a shovel and worked on the drift. 'I will tell you something,' he said after five minutes of shovelling.

'What?'

'Just because two people speak the same language, it doesn't mean they understand each other.'

'The tourists and the Tuareg?'

He nodded. 'If I learned the language of cat, I would not think like a cat.'

It was still rather early for philosophy.

Fouad let out a kind of grunting sound. 'A hundred years ago our worlds were separated,' he said.

'By distance?'

'Yes. By distance. Now they are closer.'

'Much closer – a short flight.'

Fouad touched my arm, his lazy eye leering towards me.

'But they are still very far apart,' he said. 'In their minds.'

Fouad's car was one of the reasons I moved to Morocco.

In Europe or the United States, it would have been condemned a generation before. There would be a hundred laws against it. Merely looking at it would get you arrested. But for the proud people of M'hamid, it was in fine roadworthy condition. Just about everything that could be torn out or smashed by human strength had been ravaged.

There were no wing mirrors or windows, dials or carpeting, and the only seat was the one the driver used. Fouad told me he had bought the vehicle cheap on account of the noise. He asked if I knew the way to the salt lake. I shook my head.

'I will drive you,' he said.

We set off.

I huddled in the cavity where the passenger seat had once been. Fouad, cloaked in his long blue robes, sat beside me, the wheel gripped tight in his hands. The engine noise was jarring beyond words, matched only by the smog we left in our trail.

There was something a little disconcerting about heading off into an ocean of sand, especially into the Sahara – the widest desert on Earth, which stretches from the Nile Valley all the way to the Atlantic. Most of us are road people. We don't realize it, but we are wedded to the notion of having tarmac beneath the wheels. Driving on sand is rather like driving over snow. You aim the vehicle in the vague direction you want to go and hope that you don't get stuck.

Fouad pointed out the tracks left by a thousand sand surfers.

'They go to the high dunes,' he said angrily. 'These tracks will be here for ever.'

I asked him about camels. I had seen very few.

'The Tuareg aren't interested in them now,' he said.

'Why?'

'Because they don't have a clutch pedal.'

An hour after leaving M'hamid we were adrift, sand all around. I quickly understood why the Bedouin call the desert *sahel* – 'sea'. To my eyes, each track was the same. But Fouad knew better. He said he could smell the dry salt lake.

'But it's miles away.'

'It rained a week ago.'

'So?'

'So I can smell the salt.'

'What does it smell like?'

'Like the ocean.'

Another hour and we came to a kind of encampment. A low stockade had been crafted expertly from thorns and was guarded by a thirsty-looking dog. It went wild at the noise of the car and came running out, its legs a blur of movement. Its master called it to heel.

We got down.

Fouad said the place was a sacred spring.

'Drink the water and you will remember.'

'Remember what?'

'Anything that ever happened to you.'

'How much does it cost?'

Fouad shot a line of words at the dog's owner. A mouth filled with big white teeth said a number.

'Thirty *dirhams*.'

'Give me a cup.'

A home-made bucket was lowered down into the well. It was a long time before we caught the sound of wood touching water.

'It's deep,' I said.

'But the water is low. I have not seen it this low.'

'Have you drunk it?'

Fouad said he had.

'Did you remember everything?'

'Yes. Every detail.'

The bucket was swung up and passed to me. Its water smelled of sewage.

'How much do I have to drink?'

'As much as you want.'

I took a gulp and swilled it round my mouth. It tasted of sewage, too. I would have spat it out, but the Tuareg seemed proud of their sacred spring and I didn't want to upset them.

Fouad leaned towards me.

'What can you remember?'

I thought back. I was sitting cross-legged on the floor playing with a little garage and a toy car, making the sound of the engine with my lips. How old was I... three, four? Then I was running through the woods, my hands filled with chestnuts, pricked by their shells. After that I was in a rose garden, riding my red bicycle between the flower beds.

'I remember my childhood,' I said.

'Drink some more of the water,' said Fouad.

It tasted foul, but I forced down another gulp, closed my eyes and thought back. I was in Morocco, in the Sahara. My mother was knitting and my sisters were nearby playing leapfrog in the sand. I looked around. My father was sitting by himself. He seemed sad. I went over. He picked up a fist of sand and let it drain through his fingers.

'We are basket weavers,' he said. 'That's what we do, we weave baskets. My father weaved baskets before me and his father before him. Tahir Jan, take pride in the baskets you weave.'

Fouad claimed the water had helped my memory.

'I don't think it was the water,' I said.

'It always works.'

'No, these memories were already inside me.'

We left the encampment, the sacred spring and the ferocious dog, and drove on across the flat surface of sand. The recent rain had brought shoots and the odd patch of green. The only flourishing plants had succulent round green pods, the size of oranges. I asked Fouad if they were good to eat.

'Touch them and you will go blind,' he said.

Two more hours and we came to a vast salt pan. A white crust stretched as far as the eye could see. There was no water, although in the middle the salt was darker, no doubt moistened by the rain.

'This is the lake,' said Fouad.

'The salt! It's the salt I have to get!'

I was overcome with a frail rally of emotion. I got down, fell to my knees and scooped up a handful of the salt crystals. There was a plastic bag in my pocket. I took it out and filled it half full.

'Shall we go?' said Fouad.

We looked at each other and then I scanned the desert. I could see from one horizon to the next. There wasn't another human in sight. I felt foolish. The journey from Casablanca had taken me to a distant destination, only to spend a moment there. I was as bad as the tourists I so disdain, who travel to India's Taj Mahal, to the Eiffel Tower or to Big Ben, snap a photo and leap back on to the tour bus.

'You have the salt,' said Fouad. 'You can go back to Casablanca.'

'I would rather spend a night in the desert,' I said.

We drove a little further to a crested sand dune, with a clutch of thorn trees on its leeward side. It was early afternoon. The sun was extremely bright. I couldn't understand how the Tuareg went without sunglasses.

Fouad laughed at the thought.

'You people need much more than we do,' he said.

'But sunglasses just make life more comfortable.'

'Comfort... comfort is from your world,' said Fouad.

He gathered some sticks and tossed them in a heap, ready for dusk. Then he joined me in the shade. I asked him how the Tuareg spent their time doing nothing. He didn't reply for a long time.

'We listen to the sounds,' he said at length.

'To the silence?'

'There is never silence.'

'But how can you stand having no books, no television, or internet?'

Fouad grinned. 'When life is too quiet, we talk.'

'Do you tell stories?'

'Sometimes.'

'Can you tell me one?'

'You like stories?'

'I'm sort of collecting them,' I said.

Fouad leaned back and the shadow of a gnarled branch fell over his face.

'I can tell you the "Tale of Hatim Tai",' he said.

I closed my eyes and the stage of my imagination was set.

'Long ago in Arabia,' said Fouad, 'there lived a wise and powerful king. His name was Hatim Tai and he was loved by every man, woman and child in the land. In his stables were the finest stallions, and in his tents the very softest carpets were laid. Hatim Tai's name was called from the rooftops and tales of his generosity filled the tea houses. Everyone in the kingdom was content, well fed and proud.

'Whenever they saw the king's cortège riding through the streets, the people bowed down. And if anyone needed to ask a favour they could do so, and their great monarch always granted whatever they asked.

'News of Hatim Tai's generosity spread far and wide and reached the ears of a neighbouring king. He was called Jaleel.

'One day, unable to take the stories any longer, he sent a messenger all dressed in black to the court of Hatim Tai. The messenger handed over a proclamation. It read: "O King Hatim Tai, I am master of a far greater land than yours, with a stronger army and far richer treasure store. I will descend upon your kingdom and kill every man, woman and child, unless you surrender immediately."

'Hatim Tai's advisers all clustered around. "We will go to war with the evil Jaleel," said the grand vizier, "for every fighting man would gladly lay down their life for you."

'King Hatim Tai heard his vizier's words. Then he raised a hand. "Listen, my courtiers," he said. "I am the one Jaleel has demanded. I cannot allow my people to face such terror. So I shall allow him to take my kingdom."

'Packing a few dates and nuts in a cloth, Hatim Tai set off to seek shelter in the mountains as a dervish. The very next day, the conquering warriors swept in, with Jaleel at their head.

'The new king installed himself in the palace and offered a ransom for anyone who would bring him Hatim Tai dead or alive. "How could you trust a king who would run away like this," he shouted from the palace walls, "rather than stand and fight like a man?"

'Hatim Tai wore the dress of a peasant and lived a simple existence in the mountains, surviving on berries and wild honey. There was no one who would ever have turned him in to Jaleel's secret guard, for they loved him so.

'Months passed and still there was no sign of Hatim Tai. Then one day Jaleel decided to hold a feast. At the festivities he doubled the ransom. He stood up and scorned the memory of Hatim Tai, declaring again that the generous king had run off rather than face battle. No sooner had he finished than a child stood up and shouted:

"Evil King Jaleel, our good King Hatim Tai disappeared to the mountains rather than spill a drop of our blood." Jaleel fell into his chair. Even now he was a hermit, Hatim Tai was showing compassion.

'Jaleel doubled the ransom for the wise king, declaring that anyone who could capture him would be buried in gold. At the same time, he raised taxes and forced all the young men into his army and many of the young women into his harem.

'Hatim Tai was gathering berries in the mountains near the cave he had made his home when he saw an old man and his wife, gathering sticks. The old man said to his wife: "I wish Hatim Tai was still our king, because life under Jaleel is too hard. The tax, the price of goods in the market. It is all too much to bear."

'"If only we could find Hatim Tai," said his wife, "then we could end our days in luxury."

'At that moment, Hatim Tai jumped out before them and pulled off his disguise. "I am your king," he said. "Take me to Jaleel and you will be rewarded with the ransom."

'The old couple fell to their knees. "Forgive

my wife, great king," said the old man. "She never meant to say such a terrible thing."

'Just then, the royal guards came upon the group and arrested them all. They found themselves in front of Jaleel in chains. "Who are these peasants?" he cried.

'"Your Highness," said the old man, "allow me to speak. I am a woodcutter and I was in the mountain forest with my wife. Seeing our poverty, King Hatim Tai revealed himself to us and ordered us to turn him in, in exchange for the ransom."

'King Hatim Tai stood as tall as his chains would allow. "It is right," he said. "This old couple discovered me. Please reward them with the ransom as you promised you would."

'King Jaleel could not believe the depth of Hatim Tai's generosity. He ordered the king to be unchained. Kneeling down before him, he gave back his throne and swore to protect him until the end of his days.'

When Fouad had finished the story, he hunched his shoulders and stared at the fire's flames. It was almost dusk. The first star showed itself, glinting like an all-seeing eye above. On

Earth there was the call of a wild dog far away. Lying there on a blanket, cloaked in darkness, I understood how the *Arabian Nights* had come about. Campfire flames fuelled my imagination, as they had done throughout history for the desert tribes.

Fouad pressed his right hand to his heart.

'I love the story of Hatim Tai very much,' he said. 'On some nights when I am here alone, with a small fire to keep me warm, I tell myself that story. Each time I hear it, I feel a little more at peace.'

He took a pinch of the salt I had collected and sprinkled it on the ground, to keep the jinns at bay.

'When I have heard it,' he said, 'I sit here and think what a good man King Hatim Tai must have been.'

'Do you think the story's true?'

'Yes.'

'Why?'

'Because it is truth.'

From *In Arabian Nights*

With Clarissa

AT DAWN WE rose and loaded the mules.

It was pouring with rain. I slipped on my poncho, and Samson wriggled into his bin-liner. We were just about to head off, when four men approached us. They said that they had decided to come with us.

'Aren't they frightened?'

The men, all in their early twenties, looked petrified, but one of them spoke for the others.

'It is time for the fear to end,' he said.

They each took the reins of a mule and led the way towards the mountain. The rest of us followed behind. As it was still dark I walked beside Clarissa. After an hour of trudging uphill, the first glint of light brought life to the undergrowth. The mist was low, hanging over Tullu Wallel like a death cloud, but I found myself stirred with new energy. At last, our motley band of mules and men had been transformed into a fully fledged expedition.

We headed straight for the mountain, which seemed to beckon us towards it. The rain didn't let up for a minute, which made the going very slow. I stayed at the back of the procession. I might have been the inspiration behind the expedition, but I was a novice at muleteering. We crossed fields and forded rivers, but we didn't seem to get any nearer to Tullu Wallel. I began to wonder if the mountain was a mirage, alluring yet unreachable.

Tadesse stopped three times during the morning to adjust the leather straps that bound the packs and saddles to the mules. In the rain the thongs stretched and had to keep being tightened. Clarissa's reins were tied to my hand and she battled on beside me. Samson was less appreciative of the experience. His blisters had got worse and I could tell that he was missing his girlfriend and Addis Ababa greatly.

For most of human history, man has walked with animals. Nothing is more natural, but the last century has erased our communal knowledge of that past. Now we think of wheels and tyres rather than legs and hooves; we think of miles per gallon and engines overheating, not of hay and animal fatigue. An internal combustion engine may be one of man's greatest achievements, but it is a noisy, polluting beast of a thing. Spend a few days trekking with pack mules through the forests of western Ethiopia, and you realize there's no comparison.

The woodland began quite suddenly. We forded a stream and ascended a steep bank, with Tadesse's sons jabbing their sticks angrily at the mules. Before us stood the forest, like a great curtain on the edge of a stage. I knew straight away that I would emerge the other side a different man.

We entered the forest and the morning sun disappeared. I have been in thick jungle before, but even the Upper Amazon couldn't compare with this. I stared up at the tops of the trees. They formed an unbroken canopy above us, each tree rising from a snarl of roots and mud, their long, vine-covered trunks rearing up into a sea of green.

The smell changed too. There was the scent of wild garlic, and the musty aroma of moss and leaf mould. There was lemon mint as well, which grew wild. I chewed it and found it helped stave off thirst. We moved in a single file, stumbling over roots and low branches, and slipping and sliding in the mud. The track wound round trees and up and down gullies, zigzagging back and forth. The four local men said they had never come into the forest before. Only the most courageous honey-gatherers ventured there. In some of the taller trees we saw more honey baskets trussed high in the branches. There was little time to think of the diabolic danger ahead. Our first worry was the mules.

Tadesse kept telling me to ride, but I dismounted early on after almost being garrotted by a low branch. Somehow Samson managed to stay on his mule most of the time. He had hidden talents as a horseman. Thankfully, the tree canopy high above us gave us some protection from the torrential rain, but the mud was appalling. Mules are always the butt of man's humour, but the hours we spent battling through the muddy floor of the forest proved to me their extraordinary worth, and I found myself appreciating the writings of Dervla Murphy more than ever. An old hand with mules, she has trekked over mountain ranges and through forests with them, but to read her you would never guess just how difficult such a feat is.

The mud had been up to our thighs for a

couple of hours, but we soldiered on. I noticed that the mules had an uncanny ability to find the best route, and Tadesse's sons encouraged me to let Clarissa find her own way. But by late morning, even Clarissa was finding the mud tough going.

I suggested that we unpack the animals and carry some of the equipment ourselves. Tadesse balked at the idea. He seemed to thrive on the mules' discomfort.

'People will not be able to say that my animals are weak now!' he shouted.

Leading pack mules through thigh-deep mud is a slow business. I wanted to try another route, but the local men said there was no other track leading to Tullu Wallel. Their certainty surprised me, especially as none of them had actually been to the mountain before. I was also worried about the ermoli tick. De Prorok had written that it worms its way under a mule's skin and lays its eggs there. If not extracted, it can cause a terrible infection.

From *In Search of King Solomon's Mines*

The Terrible One

MOST TOURISTS WHO venture to the Peruvian Amazon love the idea of the jungle.

They want it just like they saw it on TV – a place which can be muted or switched off by a remote control. Some expect nothing less than air-conditioning, a mini-bar, laundry service, and satellite television. Fortunately for them, there are a variety of 'jungle' lodges with such amenities a stone's throw from Iquitos. Few foreigners are willing to endure the kind of exacting expedition which Richard Fowler leads. The rough reality of his journeys wards away most civilians. He said that the US military sometimes ask him to train elite SEAL units in jungle survival. Infrequent adverts placed in *Soldier of Fortune* bring him a few more battle-hardened adventurers, tough enough to withstand what he calls the *real* jungle.

The difference between Richard and the others, and me, was that they understood the rain forest. They loved it. They were a part of it. As far as I was concerned that abyss of green was something to fear; something to despise.

From the moment I took my first jungle steps, it sensed an intruder had violated its boundary. I was soon drenched with sweat, my mouth cold and rasping, parched beyond words. I followed in Richard's size eleven footprints, focusing on them and nothing else.

Let your eyes strain too closely at a branch or twig, and you start seeing the hideous detail. With fear, the jungle closes in, the insects get bigger, magnified by the mind. How could Richard have prowled through the forests of Vietnam, hunting and being hunted at the same time?

When I asked him, he told me to concentrate on the five rules of jungle travel. One: chop stems downward and as low to the ground as possible; then they'll fall away from the path. Two: go slow, as speed only snags you on fish-hook thorns. Three: rest frequently and drink liquid. Four: love the jungle, don't hate it. Five: check your groin for parasites twice an hour.

Our Shuar companions must have thought it was mad. Whenever we stopped, I'd pull down my trousers and forage about in my boxer shorts. The area was inflamed by chafing and sweat. But there were no bugs. To tell the truth, I didn't really know what parasites to expect. I'd seen some cocoons which Richard had eaten, and plenty of roaches and wolfies, but surely they were too big to nestle comfortably in my crotch. Richard said any self-respecting grub would want to burrow into my private parts – it's what they are programmed to do. I told him of the inflammation and the chafing.

'The rawer and bloodier it is down there,' he said, 'the snugger the larvae will be.'

We marched on, but the chafing only got worse. I tried lubricating the area with Vaseline. Then I sprinkled it with mentholated foot powder. But a dark purple rash developed. Alberto asked to see the inflammation. While Enrique held the sloth, the shaman scraped a fingernail over the rash. He made a clicking sound, tramped off into the jungle, and returned with a mass of foliage. Then he rubbed the thin milky sap from the leaves onto the inflammation. The itching was soothed immediately. A couple of hours later, the rash was gone.

'*Huayra caspi*,' said Richard. 'It's a tree with

red bark; the milk eases irritations. It's especially good for venereal disease.'

We moved forward for another hour or so, until about four o'clock. Then Alberto said we should camp for the first night.

'*First* night? How far is Ramón's village?'

The shaman fed the sloth a clump of *cecropia* leaves.

'Two or three nights more,' he said.

I sat on a sheet of plastic while Richard built a basic shelter from branches of *yarena* palm. I dared not move. The Shuars had never been to a city, but they knew I was a city type. My hands weren't scarred like theirs, and I jumped at any sound. They enjoyed my reaction to giant spiders most. I whimpered when I saw them. All around in the darkness spiders' eyes reflected my torchlight, thousands of them, glinting like pearls. Pink-toed tarantulas were everywhere. They were out hunting. Richard caught one and tried to make me watch as it scurried over his face and his back. He drew my reluctant attention to the tips of their legs, which looked as though they had been coated neatly with pretty pink nail varnish.

I wondered how I would go on. Nature had become my tormentor. I had begun to regard it with absolute loathing. But then I spotted something wonderful squatting on a low branch. It was a frog, like none I'd seen before. Its skin, which glistened as if coated with lacquer, was indigo blue, marbled with splotches of black. Most of the other animals I had come across were timid, expecting imminent death. The indigo frog was far more self-assured. He sat on his branch, looking out at the green world.

So impressed was I with the little creature's confidence, I told Richard to come and have a look. He wiped his machete on his fatigues and peered down at the frog.

'*Dendrobates azureus*,' he mumbled, 'they're fuckin' wild suckers.'

'What's wild about 'em?'

'Poison arrow frogs,' he said. 'When they get stressed they secrete nerve toxins onto their skin. Any predator not warded off by the bright colours gets floored.'

As far as Richard was concerned, the indigo frog was dangerous but not unfriendly. The reptile's yellow cousin, living over in the jungles of Surinam, was another story altogether.

'They call it *Phyllobates terriblis*,' he mumbled, 'the *terrible* one.'

'*Terrible*!'

'They've got enough toxins to kill twenty thousand mice. They look like glazed lemons. They're kings of the jungle.'

While we were admiring the indigo frog, Enrique strode over. Before I could stop him, he jabbed a sliver of sharpened stick through the reptile's neck, until it came out its back. The creature didn't die, but exuded a thick foam onto its back. Mindful not to touch the frog, the Shuar chief dipped three or four darts into the foam. Then he headed away into the jungle with the dogs.

By the time the shelter was completed, it was getting dark. The fluorescent green of glow-worms glimmered in the undergrowth, hinting at secret life. Alberto helped me find some rotting wood to feed the beetles. The smaller one looked very forlorn, its powerful mandibles uninterested in crushing any food. I considered tossing the *Titanus giganticuses* back into the jungle then and there. But, unfortunately for them, they'd become pawns in a despicable human game. Too much money was at stake, and I still hoped to recoup my funds. I whispered to them that in Tokyo or in New York a big bug lover was waiting to pamper them.

Alberto told me to skewer the beetles on a spike and roast them. He said they tasted nutty, like Brazil nuts. At that moment Enrique stepped from the undergrowth, his blowpipe in one hand, a young *paca* in the other.

We lit a fire and roasted the *paca* on a spit. The flames lit up the night, shooting sparks into the trees. The smoke, and the smell of charred meat, kept the insects away. I was in no mood for another rodent meal, so I sprinkled a few grains of *Ajinomoto* powder onto my tongue and thought of roast beef. As I had expected Ramón to live close to the river, I hadn't brought much equipment. With no insect repellent or sleeping-bag, and little drinking water, I prepared myself for a torturous night.

I hunkered down beneath the shelter, praying for the giant insects, the snakes and the poison-arrow frogs to keep away. Richard slept soundly, snoring beside me. Alberto and Enrique bedded down on a natural platform in a *lapuna* tree, making mattresses of its dark green foliage. As I tried to sleep, I cautioned myself never to return to the jungle. This, the real experience, was the preserve of the professionals. People like me should stay at home and watch it on TV.

The morning was slow in coming. Only when the last shadows had been wrung from the night did the first stream of sunlight break through the canopy. I started the day by checking for genital intruders. The tips of my fingers had mastered the art of probing for maggots and chrysalids. I poked about, still half-asleep. Something was lodged there. As I tried to extract it, it turned into mush.

'Hope it wasn't burrowing,' said Richard. 'If there's still some in there, you're up shit creek.'

Reluctantly, I allowed the Vietnam vet to inspect the area. The last thing I wanted was a grubby GI rooting about in my boxer shorts.

Richard identified the problem. He said something had indeed been burrowing into my upper thigh. He suspected it was the larva of a chigger mite (the organism that Nicole Maxwell had dabbed with scarlet nail varnish to destroy). Alas, we had no nail varnish. I asked Richard for more information.

He gave me an uneasy glance and looked away.

'Of course, there's always the possibility,' he said delicately, 'that it's not going in, but coming out.'

I grimaced.

'It might be a guinea worm boring to the surface,' he said. 'But let's hope it's not that.'

'Why? What's wrong with guinea worms?'

'By the time they're boring to the surface,' said Richard, 'they've reproduced, filling you with millions of larvae.'

We dabbed the area with clinical alcohol and foot powder, and hoped for the best. Then it was time to move on.

From *Trail of Feathers*

Into the Great Thar

IGOR SINGH LED his camels to Hotel Paradise long before the sun had broken across the horizon. Prideep tried to wash pigeon droppings from his face in the blackness.

The two she-camels were very old. Igor kept kicking them to show their sturdiness. It was something which they did not appreciate at three am. We walked down through the town and out along a desert path. Igor Singh had no torch. When I gave him mine, he held it close to his chest, expecting it to become a gift. I held onto Igor's shirt-tail, Osman clutched onto mine, with Prideep stumbling somewhere behind him. It seemed as if we were casualties of some horrific war, blinded by gas.

By the time streams of yellow light appeared from the sky, we were quite far from the city walls. The yellow sandstone of Jaisalmer stood invisible within the rays. Our band stopped every so often to drink water from a goatskin. The camels would sit, their legs turned inwards, and their giant lashes fanning over golf ball eyes.

Their names were Unt, meaning 'camel', and Qaisara, which means 'empress'.

Igor Singh was a disciplined man who would let neither his animals nor his guests relax for long. Covering our heads with shirts, we swaggered with exaggerated movements towards the horizon. Osman read bearings from the compass, pretending that we were tracking treasure with a map. But we had no map. It struck me that our guide could easily slit our throats, steal our money and belongings and still return to town before breakfast.

It was odd that a Sikh should, firstly, be in Jaisalmer and, secondly, have a Russian first name. Igor began to speak, Osman translated his words so that I might understand the life of this peculiar man.

'My father came to Rajasthan between the world wars. He was sick of Russia, the country of his birth, so he escaped communism and he decided to live in India. He married a Punjabi girl who was working in Jaipur. After Partition and all the slaughter accompanying the splitting of India and Pakistan in the mid-1940s, they wanted to get away from people and so they moved to Jaisalmer. I was brought up here.'

'Do you speak Russian?' I asked.

'I am a mixture, so have all the advantages of a crossbreed. I taught myself about my mother's Sikh religion. And, as I am out here much of the time, it doesn't bother me to wear a turban.'

Osman and Prideep climbed on Unt's back and I was offered Qaisara. The she-camels groaned as we ascended. I was immediately gripped by motion sickness. Qaisara's gait made it like riding in the wispy shell of a boat through rough sea. Prideep was thrilled by the new experience. Enjoying his adventure away from Bombay, from time to time he reminisced to Osman, and speculated on the gossip which our trip must have provoked.

Qaisara sighed, I guessed in relief, as her parasite population seeped onto me. And, by early afternoon, there was nothing in front of us, and nothing behind, but sand. I had grown used to the idea of being in the Great Thar Desert: the novelty had quickly worn off.

We stumbled along all day under a sun which

made our faces raw. My camel bags were at last in their native environment, much less of a burden to me, thrown over Qaisara's bony back. I wondered for a moment if my grandfather's expedition through the desert had been similar to mine. Perhaps one of his journeys had been across these very plains. Perhaps he, too, had gone in search of treasure in the Great Thar Desert.

There was no sign that it had rained in the desert. Thoughts of the camel drowning occupied me for at least an hour. Then, images of a chest brimming with rubies replaced those of floundering camels. My pace quickened and my mouth salivated with greed.

Osman began to shout. 'I see People! People!'

Rubbing the sand from my eyes, I turned round 360 degrees. Still I could see no movement. Prideep leapt about as if suddenly illuminated. He and Osman embraced like old comrades reuniting.

'What the hell are you talking about? There's nothing, you idiots!' I yelled, fearing that they had both finally cracked.

'There! Look over there!'

Osman placed his hand on mine and pointed. He was right. There, in the distance, was a tiny speck which looked like a flea, jumping about. Then others. My brain and all its contents seemed to have been erased. I could just about understand fleas and sand. The thought of a city or of driving a car seemed terrifying. Would I be able to live in Western society again?

The specks grew bigger. They were not fleas, and dogs could be seen running about their feet. Was it Mandha, the place where Abdul lived? Yes, Igor assured us, it was.

Qaisara and Unt were given to a child to look after. Igor Singh led us to a group of desert folk. The men, each with a full beard and a face worn by the harsh conditions, sat in a circle around a smouldering campfire. The greetings were formal and drawn out. I prodded Igor to find out if Abdul was around.

'Tell me! Is Abdul the Warrior here?' Igor paused and parted his chapped lips.

'Yes, the Warrior is in Mandha.'

'Has he the treasure?'

'Yes, he has it at his house.'

107

'Could we go straight there?'

Yes, indeed we could.

Abdul the Warrior had the physique of a bear. His face was hidden by a massive black beard: only his great hook of a nose seemed to escape the bristles. His back was rounded, and his immense hands shot forward as I drew near. The Warrior pulled me to his chest like a long-lost son being welcomed by his father. He did not mention the treasure. I knew that it would be impolite to ask of it before we ate.

Dates were brought and straw-coloured tea was poured into dainty cups. Abdul grinned ferociously, and sipped from the white china, which he held in his thumb and forefinger like an upturned thimble.

Three chickens had been roasted and buried in a bed of *pilau* rice. I fished for a leg. Abdul dug his hand into the mound of rice and threw a whole chicken across to me. He growled. I grasped at the bony feet and sunk my teeth into the breast. The Warrior seemed pleased and, rubbing his fingers into the thick mass of black bristle that sprouted from his face, he spoke. Everyone listened.

'You are friends of Yusuf Jahan?'

'Yes, Sir. He sent us to meet you. We travelled from the busy streets of Bombay, across Gujarat and Rajasthan in search of you. The Dervish said that perhaps you might help us on our quest.'

Abdul stopped me as I spoke: he obviously had some advance information.

'I understand that you seek the great treasures of the world.'

'Yes, Sir.' I shifted apprehensively. 'Do you have anything here that might be of interest?'

'You may see what I have, my humble possessions. I insist that you take any which are to your liking.'

Abdul signalled to one of his men who was weighted down by bandoliers and endless rounds of heavy-calibre ammunition. A tea-chest was carried in by two other men. My heart beat faster and faster. More dates were passed around. A pack of dogs began to bark outside.

Abdul reached for the chest. He lifted the lid off. I rubbed the vision of rubies from my eyes, peering into the darkness of the box. Osman and I gagged at its contents. Prideep pushed us aside so that he, too, might see the riches. Abdul was pleased with our speechlessness. He delved his great fingers into the tea-chest and pulled out the most grotesque coloured glass lampshade that I had ever seen.

A paraffin lamp was brought closer, and the Warrior ran his fingertips over an engraving.

'Can you read what it says?' he roared.

I held the lampshade under the light and read out the legend:

'Made in Birmingham.'

Abdul the Warrior winced with delight and gasped, 'Do you know how far away that is?'

'Yes, Sir. It is many miles from the Great Thar Desert,' I said.

'Would you like it?'

Abdul was prepared to offer it as a gift. There was silence. Images of sand and fleas danced around in my mind as I tried to string a set of words together.

'*Aga-i Janab*, Respected Sir,' I began, 'you are a lucky man indeed to own such a valuable object. Fate favours us both, having extended great fortune to me also. For I already have an identical lampshade to this. It is destiny that has given us both such a wondrous thing.'

Abdul the Warrior had tears of empathy in his eyes. In the desert there is little beauty but there is a closeness and solidarity between all men. Abdul looked at Osman, Prideep and I, and said, very softly:

'My boys, stay here and live with me. It is my honour to be your host.'

From *Beyond the Devil's Teeth*

The Man Whose Arms Grew Branches

MANY LIFETIMES AGO, the tree began, I was a child, a human child in my native Iceland.

I used to run through the fields and the forests, and play with my brothers and sisters in the long summer days. The world was perfect then, and we used to be thankful for the warmth on our faces, and for the soft ground beneath our feet.

But most of all, we were thankful for the trees.

We would climb them, carve our names on their trunks, swing from them, and lie in their branches, talking of all the adventures we would have in the years ahead.

One summer evening, I climbed to the very top of a soaring beech tree, and looked out over the forest. The view was astonishing – a carpet of green, an immensity that could never be dominated, even by Man.

Or so I thought.

Years passed and, before I knew it, I was no longer a child – but an adult with a wife and children of my own. However hard I worked in the town I never had enough money to make ends meet. My wife used to scold me, declaring that I didn't strive hard enough in the market. My problem was that there just wasn't enough work.

Then, one day, I overheard a wealthy man telling a stall-keeper that he had made a fortune in the timber business. He had got the right to chop down trees in a land to the west of our own. My ears pricked up, because the thought of being in the countryside, and gaining real wealth, was extremely interesting.

The next thing I knew, I had become a woodcutter.

I bought the very best axe I could afford, and chopped down trees from morning until night. I was strong and athletic, and found that I could do the job far better than anyone else.

Within a few months, I had paid my debts and had cleared a huge swathe of forest. And, within a couple of years, I was rich, and my wife was dressed in fine satins and silks.

But, as is the way of women, she wanted more. And more, and more.

So, I kept chopping, cutting down all the

trees I found in my path – great big trees and tiny saplings. Nothing escaped my blade.

One morning, as I was unsheathing my axe deep in the forest where I was camping, a little turquoise bird flew down and perched on my shoulder.

'Please stop chopping down our forest,' said the bird in my ear. 'All the birds and the other animals are suffering because of you. If you don't stop, the forest will take revenge.'

Swishing the little creature away, I got down to my work and, that day alone, I hacked down thirty trees.

Time slipped by and I made more and more money – so much so that I hired a team of woodcutters and got them to work for me. We bought better and better axes and, each week, I became more wealthy. But, needless to say, my wife found ways to spend all the money I earned.

Then, one morning, I woke up with a pain in my hand. I assumed it was from years of chopping wood, and so I rested.

A few days passed, and a pain began bothering my other hand. A week on, and something very strange indeed happened.

A little shoot began to sprout from my elbow.

Naturally, I was very alarmed. I showed it to my wife. Screaming, she sent me to a doctor, and left to visit her mother in the neighbouring town.

The doctor prescribed a tonic, and told me to get rest. So I took to my bed for a week, drinking the tonic morning and night.

As I lay there, under the blanket, the shoot began to grow.

It grew and it grew, and it grew and it grew, until it was more of a branch than a simple shoot. And, at the same time, another shoot sprouted on my other elbow, and on both my hands. Before I knew it, there were shoots peeping out from each finger, and from my ears as well.

I was terrified and ashamed.

No one else I knew had foliage growing from their body. After three weeks, my wife came back from her mother's home. By this time, my entire frame was covered in greenery. Vines were growing out of my nostrils and my face was rough and grey like the trunk of a tree.

And that is what I was becoming – an oak tree.

My wife ordered me to leave the house at

once. She said I was bewitched and that I had brought dishonour to our home. Confused and humiliated, I set off, to get away from people. Whenever anyone saw me, they taunted me, calling me an oddity and a freak.

And then, one day, I reached the forest where we now find ourselves.

By that time I had lost the use of my arms, with branches in their place. My torso was more like a tree's trunk than a human body and, with each moment, I felt my legs stiffen a little more. As for my toes, they had become roots, roots searching for soft ground in which to plant themselves. I knew deep down in my sap why this change in circumstances had come.

It was retribution from the forest for having felled so many fine trees with my axe.

The oak tree paused for a moment as a light breeze rippled through its leaves.

He seemed to sigh.

All this happened centuries ago, he said. And I suppose I should be thankful because I have outlived all the people I have ever known.

The tree sighed again.

I wish I could do something – anything – he said, to teach other humans to change the path of their ways.

Yousef, who had listened to the tree's story, touched a hand to the oak's great trunk.

'I have come to know the secret of humanity,' he said, 'and I am devoting what time I have left to making this knowledge available to all men.'

The oak tree rustled with interest.

'Would you tell me the secret?' he asked.

And so Yousef explained all he had come to understand.

When he was finished, the oak tree was overcome.

'I wish I had grasped such a simple and important lesson when I was still a human,' he replied.

The next morning, Yousef thanked the tree for his shelter, and the tree lowered a twig for him to shake.

Just as he turned to go, the tree made the sound like the clearing of his throat.

'I have been thinking,' he said humbly, 'and I want to help you.'

Yousef frowned.

'What do you mean?' he said. 'I don't want to sound rude, but you are a tree. How could you help me with my cause?'

The tree said:

'Last night you explained to me your quest, and for it you will have to spread the word to men. This secret needs to be passed on, and on.'

Yousef nodded.

'But how can you help me, dear tree?'

The oak seemed to stand a little taller and prouder than before.

'From my branches you can make paper,' he said, 'and from my twigs you can fashion a nib. From the oak apples in my high branches you can make ink. And,' he said, his voice quivering slightly, 'when you are done creating a book from me, you can make a beautiful box from my trunk in which to keep that book.'

Yousef took in the mighty oak's wide trunk, its branches, its twigs, leaves and shoots.

'Dear oak, I could not betray your kindness,' he said.

The oak replied:

'Even after I have betrayed the forest, among which I have now lived for an eternity. Cut me down, and I shall begin life in a new form.'

And so, a tear in his eye, Yousef cut down the tree.

He made paper from its twigs, and ink from the oak apples, and sewed the binding with twine. Once he had created a huge tome, standing as tall as a man, he created a magnificent chest to contain it, delicately carved and scented with the fragrance of the forest.

And, on the front of the chest, he inscribed the following words:

My form may have changed once, and then again, but I contain the wisdom of all Men.

The chest was then heaved onto a grand cart, and transported to the National Library, where it was given as a gift to all the people of the land.

A few days after the great book arrived at the library, the kingdom was overthrown by an invading army. Much of the population were slaughtered, including Yousef. All the libraries in the kingdom were destroyed by fire, and anyone found owning a book was burned at the stake.

The invading despot gave the order for the farmland of the vanquished country to be tilled with salt. So ruthless was his new regime that the people fled to other kingdoms, their lands unfit to be ploughed, their capital destroyed. Eventually, all the people gone, nature reclaimed the ruins of the capital.

Centuries passed.

Where the capital had once stood, a forest grew, giant oaks forming an unreachable barricade against the outside world.

And then, one day, a hunter strayed into the forest on the trail of a beautiful gazelle, when he became disorientated and lost. Night fell quickly, forcing him to bed down on a rock, itself covered in moss.

Awaking the next morning, the hunter realized that he had been seeking shelter in what appeared to be the ruins of an ancient building.

Surveying the area, he found the enormous carved wooden chest, all covered in creepers and vines. Carefully, he cut away the lianas. And, with all his strength, he pushed back the lid.

Inside, perfectly protected, was a colossal book.

Intrigued at what he had discovered, the hunter forgot about the gazelle, and began to read...

From *Scorpion Soup*

Dictatorship Central

DENZIL KNEW A lot about Uganda and its history.

He told with great animation of the brutality of Idi Amin and Milton Obote, describing Uganda as 'Dictatorship Central'. And he spoke of the burial grounds where the earth was parted and filled with corpses. These were Uganda's killing-fields.

As the sun sank down behind Kampala's concrete buildings, Denzil strapped two jerrycans brimming with petrol onto the sidecar. Oswaldo and I risked instant incineration trapped in that death seat. Petrol slopped about as we set off at dawn the next day to witness the evil legacy of Amin and Obote. Although I was apprehensive – and at first unwilling – to visit the killing-fields, Denzil maintained that such a trip would be of significance.

For several hours we drove along red mud-tracks bordered with lush vegetation. Once in a while Denzil would pull out a hand-scribbled map. His up-to-date information and interest in such matters as the killing-fields led me to suppose that the lanky Englishman had unrevealed contacts: perhaps in the Foreign Office. Rather oddly, he seemed reluctant to brief Oswaldo and me as to where the killing-fields were located. When I asked him to give me names and directions for my notebook, he said firmly that these details were irrelevant. Perhaps, I reflected, I had contracted the Developing World paranoia, which almost everywhere holds that newcomers are undoubtedly spies.

At what seemed like the middle of nowhere, Denzil stopped driving, glanced at the tatty map, and switched off the engine.

'We are here,' he said.

An albino boy ran up to the motorbike and screamed when he saw Denzil.

The child plucked up courage, slowly approaching the Englishman and rubbing his fingers through Denzil's long brown hair. Then he chortled, because he had never before felt such a thing. A moment later he touched Denzil's freckles. There were cries from behind us, and the child's mother ran over. She yanked the boy up into her arms, smacked him, and rushed over to a trough to wash his hands. Denzil looked a little disconcerted. The woman had obviously never seen freckles before and thought, quite naturally, that they were due to a disease which might be contagious.

We stayed the night at the back of a teahouse. A fire burned in the middle of the little room. The flames licked at the corrugated iron walls, crackling and squeaking as the fire was fed with a few old pieces of damp wood.

The man who put us up was very old indeed. His name was Albany, and his eyes were rheumy with age. He spoke wearily, as if he had seen the history of the world and all those who had walked upon it. And he told stories of the slaughter.

Albany had seen corpses being dragged into open pits – often by the victim's own children.

In Uganda a generation was stolen by the deeds of tyrannical rule. Albany's raspy words echoed around us. As the flames licked higher than before, the old Ugandan spoke about the lost years of the second Obote reign.

Obote had returned to a people who were beginning to recover from Amin's terror; a people who had not realized that a new dictator had just replaced the last. Albany said that he would rather the truth be told just once, than it never be told at all.

Next morning Albany took us to a leper colony near to the hut in which he lived. I was not sure of the reason for visiting the enclosure and its inhabitants. At first I felt like a voyeur, or a child being taken to visit a zoo. Albany knew the lepers well and introduced us to them. Their features and bodies were actually rotting; holes had formed in cheeks, and finger-joints had dropped away.

It was the first time that I had seen serious disease since Bombay. Dry leprosy is not usually as highly contagious as people tend to believe. Oswaldo reached into his pack and pulled out a bag of boiled sweets. They were striped with white and black lines. He handed them to the oldest of the lepers. The joy was no longer expressed in physical demeanour, but in a distinctly higher sense, as if an aura surrounded him.

Few people lived in the region. Visitors were unknown. It was as if the world were trying to leave it alone, in peace.

We walked across a field to buy some milk

from a stall. What looked like thick sticks were scattered about, their ends fat and rounded. Skulls were spread about like orbs, some enmossed – others shining brightly – polished by the rain. Many of the bones and skulls were small and delicate; they were those of children and their mothers.

Albany gave us some bananas when we left. He told us to tell our friends that his country had found peace at last. And called out:

'Smile, when you think of us here, because we are smiling for the world.'

The jerrycans were secured and we mounted the black machine. The fuel was hardly the purest: clouds of noxious gases spiralled behind us as we pulled away to seek the source of the Nile.

From *Beyond the Devil's Teeth*

The Horrible Trophy

'OUR DISMAL CARAVAN departed Timbuctoo,' Robert Adams spoke loudly so that the entire audience might hear, 'and pushed north into the vast desert of the Zahara.

'We were like a parade of ants marching with purpose over a field of sand. As I trudged forward in chains, I made an oath that if I were ever able, I would return to the desert city and serve King Woolo with his due. But then, as I pondered it, my flayed bare feet tramping over sand, the Lord is the ultimate scale of justice. He sees every deed and misdeed, and it is He who metes out judgement when the right time has come.

'So we walked, and we walked, and we walked – the first horizon followed by fifty more. The manacles on my wrists and ankles cut deep into the flesh, and the lacerations turned to sores. When I shouted out in pain, the Moorish commander howled with laughter, and offered to remove my hands and feet to relieve my discomfort.

'Leaving the agreeable lodgings of Timbuctoo

took a toll on both Sanchez and me. We had grown used to sleeping on smooth mattresses, and to eating as much as our stomachs could take. In a way I was content though, however severe the curse of crossing that emptiness. For I knew that the only way of returning to Christina was by placing one foot squarely in front of the last. Sitting in the court of that despot there was but one assurance – of never setting eyes again on my wife.

'Sanchez did not share my contentment. From the moment we embarked from the mud city, his spirits became forlorn. He wept for three horizons, and was flogged for his trouble by the Moors. One night, as we lay there, watching the stars and waiting for sleep, he whispered that he would escape, and retrace his steps to Timbuctoo.

'"You will be hunted," I said. "And they will catch you. After all, how can you run with those shackles?"

'"One minute of freedom is equal to a lifetime of custody," he replied.

'"We must stay with the caravan until the desert sands subside a little," I said. "Flee now, and death is the only certainty. We must take our time and choose the moment well."

'I fell asleep gazing up at the stars. Then, suddenly, I awoke. It was the middle of the night and a great commotion had ensued. The Moors leapt to their feet, greatly enraged.

'A group of them lit fiery torches, mounted their camels, and charged into the night. I sat up to ask Sanchez what was happening.

'But he was gone.

'At dawn, the Moors returned. They climbed down from their camels and, in turn, strode over to where I was crouching. In his hand the commander clutched the grimmest trophy – Sanchez's bloodied head.

'He threw it at me.

'I held it, weeping. As I did so, the other soldiers tossed down trophies of their own – two feet and a pair of hands. I wondered how long Sanchez had lived as the Moors hacked him to pieces. But it did not matter now, for he had succeeded in escaping.

'Before the caravan moved on, I struggled to bury Sanchez's remains in the sand. As I dug ferociously with my hands, I could feel my departed friend gazing down at me. Dressed in white, unblemished by scars and blood, he was at peace. I admit it, that I contemplated running like he had done, in a bid for freedom. But something inside me stirred, and I chastised myself at contemplating what amounted to suicide.

'So we marched on, the Moors riding their camels, and I lumbering over the desert. In some places the sand was baked hard like terracotta, and in others it was rolling loose, interspersed with immense dunes.

'The Moors who had been kept prisoner in Timbuctoo were severely weakened. Their ribs were poking through their chests, their faces gaunt and their stomachs distended from starvation. The night after Sanchez had left us, one of them fell down dead. He didn't make a sound, for his body was almost weightless.

'The day after that, another two succumbed. The commander looked back, but did not give the order to stop. He was a vindictive man, who regarded Christians as vermin. Yet as a leader he was skilled. If the caravan had paused for a single moment, we would not have reached the dank waterhole that night, and the lives of the camels would have been put in danger.

'As it was, the largest of the she-camels fell to her knees in the afternoon heat. I looked round at the other beasts and, when I turned back, she was dead. I suppose her heart had simply given in. Without wasting any time at all, the Moors drained her paunch, skinned her, and cut out the meat.

'The commander fed the choicest morsels to the men who had been starved. Some of the bones were wrapped up, along with the flesh, and packed on other camels.

'We marched for another week or more. The camel meat was rationed, although I was given only the bones. I cracked them open, sucked at the marrow, and felt much the better for it.

'Another day or two passed and the meat ran out. Then two of the Moors became deranged. They ran off into the desert, howling like dogs. Although agitated, the commander chose not to save them. It seemed as if we were in the driest expanse of the great Zahara, and that survival depended on the disciplined march. I considered breaking free, doing as the Moors had done. But alone there would have been no chance of survival at all.

'Each day the commander forced more from the group. There were twenty of us now. He would start a little earlier, breaking only for Musalman prayers, and for half a mouthful of precious water every few hours.

'Then, one evening, we lay down to sleep. I was dreaming of my childhood, splashing in the river, bathing in its waterfalls. Suddenly, I was woken by a wind of astonishing force.

'It ripped over the surface of the desert, howling like Death itself. Fumbling frantically, the Moors tethered their animals and piled their bundles together. The night was moonless, but I didn't need light to sense the terrible fear.

'It was as if the world were about to end.

'An hour after first hearing the wind, it arrived – blinding, choking, suffocating man and beast. With no clothing to protect me, the skin was chafed from my back, and the hair ripped from my head. Three of the camels were buried alive, as were the men who were holding them down. The wind raged the entire night, grinding away. Pushing my face into the belly of a male camel, I prayed he would not be buried.

'By noon the following day the wind had dropped and the commander took stock of the situation. Four camels had been lost together with five men. A pair of valuable water skins had vanished, too, and a second pair were torn. Without sparing a moment, our leader gave the order to march.

'After a mile or so of walking we reached dunes again. There was no alternative but to surmount them. With the camels groaning, we ascended, and found ourselves at a vantage point, gazing down at a sight from the infernos of Hell.

'On the plain below lay the remains of an immense caravan, a caravan of death – a thousand camel skeletons, and at least twice as many men. They had been buried alive long ago, suffocated, unearthed by the sandstorm. It seemed they were destined for the Musalman city of Mecca, many months to the east.

'We tiptoed past the contorted faces and the torn, twisted skeletons. I tried not to look but, gripped by lewd fascination, I could not help myself from scanning the desiccated, tortured expressions, skin dried taut over bones.

'As I gazed at them, each one a story of grim submission, I could only wonder whether we were destined for the same horrible fate.'

From *Timbuctoo*

Deep Jungle

AFTER FOLLOWING THE watercourse for days, it was a wonderful feeling to climb above it.

Within an hour of slashing and traipsing through undergrowth, we reached a natural *mirador*. From there we got a good look at the pinnacles. There were about a dozen, all odd angular shapes, probably having fallen away from the ridge in ancient times. To get to them, we had to cut a trail in an arc, veering down to the south. Without the porters, and the equipment they bore so unhappily, we made fast progress.

Three hours after setting out, we had managed to climb one of the structures. As we ascended, the vegetation quickly changed, from trees and bamboo to ferns and other higher-altitude flora. There were orchids now, and bromeliads, and every branch and twig was encrusted with green-grey lichens. The temperature fell sharply, too. It was as if we had crossed an invisible barrier, a divide between one realm and the next.

Despite the coolness of the air, we sweated uncontrollably from exertion, and were caked with sweat bees and small black flies. They crawled over our skin and clothes, desperate to suck liquid from our dry mouths and from our eyes. With the river so close, I couldn't understand why their thirst was so great.

Near to the top of the pinnacle, we were forced to haul ourselves up over decomposing vegetation. The granite base was lost beneath many layers of dead branches and fallen trees. We used one of the static ropes, but it wasn't much good. The amateur climbers for whom they were made rarely have the inconvenience of such a deluge of roots and twisted stems.

Finally we made it to the top and surveyed the area. It was a place of astonishing natural beauty, and of some secrecy. But it lacked a key ingredient: enchantment. The Incas would have liked it there, I thought, as we went down, but they would never have constructed Paititi in such an obvious place. For them nothing was quite so important as a landscape in which they felt the enduring presence of their god.

The men reached a slender scrap of beach, and crouched on their haunches, pack straps cutting into their shoulders. They were waiting for my signal to move on. I was about to give it, but it was then that Pancho nudged a finger at the ridge and emitted the reviled word: '*Arriba.*'

Twenty-four hours later I was alone, deserted by the film crew, the porters, and Pancho. The willowy warrior had led the way up the granite rock face to the top of the ridge. He climbed nimbly, a sharp contrast to my display of wheezing and puffing. I envied him, and hated him at the same time.

At the top, we parted ways. He wasn't going on. He left as quickly as he had come. The message I got from his silence was that he wanted *me* to go on. But I would have to take the last steps by myself.

I felt sure that Pancho had brought me to the brink, but he had sworn to the tribe never to reveal the actual location of the ruins. Without him and the porters the expedition was crippled, but I knew Paititi was close. If need be, I was prepared to go on alone for days. The Swedes had begged me to turn back. They had said there was no hope. I was adamant that we were on the verge of victory.

I had all I needed to survive in a kit-bag: some plastic sheeting, matches, a machete, sleeping-bag and flashlight, a change of clothes, plenty of food and some water. Once Pancho was gone, I took stock of the situation, and made a small camp at the foot of a rubber tree. I erected a canopy, tied the corners down tight, and set about gathering wood for a fire. My only fear was of *Tremarctos ornatus*, the so-called spectacled bear, but I hoped the fire would keep them away.

To be there alone in that wilderness was the most daunting yet elevating experience. I felt *alive*, truly alive. I was almost lame, my feet severely damaged by weeks in the river, and I was ground down by the recurring fever. But at the same time I felt stronger than I ever had before.

I passed the night quite peacefully, protected by my ingenuousness. The fog lingered until first light, shrouding my camp like a muslin veil. I slept on and off, and talked to myself a great deal. When the sun was up and the air was touched by its heat, I marched on, searching for the Inca stone road or the lake. Words cannot describe the sensation. It was as if I was on top of the world, looking down across an unending carpet of trees, millions and millions of trees. I was small, and getting smaller. The jungle was massive and, with every step, it doubled in size and magnificence.

I took great care to stay in radio contact with the film crew who, along with the men, had made their way back down to the river. Every few hundred feet I put a marker in the GPS – the limit of my skill. I was wearing gloves for the first time: without them the bamboo lacerated my hands. I staggered ahead, hoping, praying, bleeding.

The highlight of the first day was the meal. I cooked two Pot Noodles and gorged myself on them. Pancho had shown me how to take water from bamboo, but still I rationed it, using the bare minimum, and became dehydrated as a result.

The lack of water probably added to my mental infirmity. By the second day my mind was raging with a ferocious anger, a madness that called for revenge. I was against the world, against humanity, against my men. I didn't give a damn about them. I wanted Paititi. I deserved it. To Hell with the rest of them. I hoped they would rot in their horrible contortion of life. I pushed on.

The trees teemed with termites and soldier ants, and monkeys howled high in the branches, baiting me, boosting my rage. There were so many monkeys, no doubt kin of the one Julio had shot and cooked. I cursed them all. The wildlife coveted by package tourists on peaceful safaris is not the same odious life-taking fauna as exists in deep jungle. *Real* wildlife is an executioner, a barbaric devourer of the dead. It was waiting for me to expire, longing to carve me up. I could sense the jungle placing bets on how long I would survive. Every ant, termite, tapir and macaw was guilty, each vying for a piece of my flesh.

As for the others, they were cowards. I cursed them, slandering their names, even those of the Swedes. Their film had destroyed my expedition. They had stifled the search, the quest, with their ludicrous luggage. In a cruel, deranged moment, I prayed that they would all lose their way home, and pass from this world to the next in the most appalling agony.

The hunt for Paititi brings out the best and the worst. But in some people, like myself, it only brought out the worst. The fuel that energized me was a blend of anger, bitterness and bile. I spat insults, cursed, begged for retribution.

On the third night alone on that mountain ridge, I squatted on the ground in misery. The fire had not caught; the wood was far too wet. The nocturnal sounds pressed close. Pancho, no doubt, would have found them comforting. To me, they were the choir of the devil. I removed my boots and unwound the bandages from my feet, anointed the skin with rubbing alcohol, and allowed the sores to touch the breeze. The sensation was soothing. One lives for such moments in times of hardship.

Crouching there, I pondered our own world, and the notion that one only knows a place by going far from it. We live in an illusion of comfort and invented luxury. We dwell on aspects of life that are framed in absolute insignificance. Such hollowness consumes us, and we forget *how* to live. The jungle was at the other extreme: a seething, accursed champion of vitality, uncontrollable and untamed.

From *House of the Tiger King*

Possession Overload

TEN MINUTES LATER we were on the road again with Bahru crunching the gears and jerking the wheel as usual, an enormous quid of *qat* stuck in his cheek.

The scenes we passed were now familiar: children with huge piles of sticks on their backs, goats being herded along the road, people trudging to distant destinations, solemn funeral processions of elders wrapped in white, making their way down mountain trails, walking in silence towards a burial ground. I asked Samson why so many people were dying.

'Life in the country is hard,' he replied. 'If you fall sick you get sicker and then you die. People with a little money use it to buy food, not medicine.'

The contrast between village life and a small town in Ethiopia is astonishing. Small Ethiopian towns are vibrant places, full of bustle. Cluttered shops sell a colourful display of goods imported from China. Boys play table tennis on the pavements. The bars are alive with deafening music, the flow of warm bottled beer and the lascivious solicitations of whores. And all the while, there is a constant flow of people arriving from the villages to barter and to buy basic necessities. In a remote village or hamlet, days from the nearest road, there are no paraffin lamps or electricity, only candles; no running water either, or shops, or the noise of an ill-tuned transistor radio. I am not new to Africa or to lands where good, innocent people are struggling to survive. Even so, I found myself reeling at the extraordinary level of hardship that rural Ethiopians endure.

Ask me to list all the things which I own and I wouldn't know where to start. I have rooms filled with stuff I never use – *Possession Overload*. Our attic is packed to bursting with objects I've collected and forgotten about. But ask a villager in the Ethiopian highlands what he has in his *tukul* and the list will be precise and short. Everything is functional and has ten uses. There's a knife, perhaps an axe, a candle or two, or a lamp made from the bottom of a tin can, a blanket and hides, a bucket, a pot, a sheet of polythene, a few old clothes, some flour and a pile of sticks. That is all.

From *In Search of King Solomon's Mines*

Temple of the Great Being

PITTZER LED THE way through the jungle into the island's hinterland, his machete chopping vines and foliage as he went.

Will, Emma and Chaudhury followed behind in single file, moving clumsily through the tangled undergrowth.

It took two more hours to reach the rocky promontory on which the temple had been built.

There was a sense life had stood still there for decades, since the stone blocks had been heaved up from the makeshift quarry below.

By the time they reached the sanctuary, they were all drenched in perspiration, their backs covered in sweat beads. Climbing up on to the outcrop, they got a clear view over the jungle and out to sea.

Pittzer halted short of the temple itself – which was another thirty feet up a granite bluff.

'This is where I leave you,' he said.

'Are you frightened?'

'You bet I am,' the anthropologist crowed. 'This is forbidden ground. Don't forget,' he said, turning, 'it's protected by hornets.'

Will touched Emma on the shoulder.

'You and Chaudhury go back with him,' he said. 'I'm doing this one alone.'

'Are you crazy? Of course we're coming!'

'I'm immune to insect stings,' Will explained. 'Don't know why, but I am.'

Emma sighed.

'I'm sure we'll be fine.'

'No,' said Will firmly. 'You've both gotta leave me. I'll see you back at the village when I'm done.'

Leaning forward, Emma hugged him, crushing his ribs.

'You take care,' she said.

'Holler if you need us, sir,' added Chaudhury.

A minute or two later, Will's boots were searching for footholds among the rocks, his fingers digging into leverage points as he scaled the bluff.

The humidity didn't make the task any easier. Stifling his breathing, it caused his head to spin. He got a flash of his great-aunts sitting in their comfy chairs back in Oakland, breathing in the scent of honeysuckle. Then, pulling himself up the last few feet, he saw his dorm room in SFSU. He had almost forgotten the life left far behind.

Cloaked in a screen of palms, the temple's ash-grey walls were overgrown in vines. Twisted and contorted, they doubled back on themselves – layers upon layers. A great monument of stone, the construction must have been fifty feet high. The rear was lost in foliage, the front bathed in stems of yellow and red heliconia flowers.

Cautiously, Will made his way towards the portal. Set in the middle, at chest height, was the sacred sign of the Garuda tribe – a symbol known to him as the monogram of Hannibal Fogg.

A little lower down, offset to the side, was a second symbol: a rectangular box bisected by a line – the Egyptian hieroglyph for 'house'.

Glancing at the back of his hand, Will looked at the lapis lazuli ring Hannibal had left him. Working out what to do, he nudged it to the hieroglyph on the door.

Nothing happened at first...

But then, very gradually, the great portal began to draw back, against a rasping sound of stone on stone.

Wedging a rock in place so that the door could not be sealed behind him, Will stepped inside.

The temple had a long, tapered hall, a wooden roof and polished stone floor. At the narrow end was a raised altar, crafted from a vast slab of pumice.

But it was the walls which caught Will's attention. Set into them, on either side of the nave, was a series of impressive stained-glass windows, through which jungle sunlight streamed.

Moving down the nave, Will took in the scenes one at a time.

The first depicted a church – not in the jungle but lodged at the top of a precipice. Beside it was a double helix: the Ladder of Mithras. The next window showed the Hands of God, set against a backdrop of human symbolism. The third portrayed the Tumi dagger of the Incas and, the fourth, the Orisha Stone.

Will turned to the opposite side of the nave, where the symbols continued.

As he stepped over to focus on the detail of

the Prayer Wheel of Kublai Khan, the temple filled with butterflies – thousands of them, cascading out from fissures in the walls.

Lost in a blizzard of multi-coloured wings, Will caught a glimpse of the blue diamond depicted in stained glass. Beyond it was a last panel.

Surrounded by Prussian-blue waves was a mask fashioned in the shape of a magnificent bird.

Another step forward and the butterflies vanished. Approaching the altar, Will wondered whether they had existed at all.

Ascending a flight of white marble steps, he reached the altar itself.

Lying on the surface of the volcanic rock was a cylindrical tube, crafted from silver.

Taking it in both hands, Will twisted it, scrutinizing the strange repeating pattern etched into the surface. For some reason it reminded him of his parents' funeral, and of the first time he had looked into Emma's eyes.

Prising off the end, he found a letter.

It was written in English in a familiar hand.

My dear William, were there more time, I would regale you with tales of how, by strange coincidence, I have become regarded as a deity in the eyes of the Garuda tribe.

But, alas, time is of the essence.

I must ask you to read the directions on the reverse of this letter only once you have reached the shrine.

Leave at once!

The reason is simple: to prevent the wrong person from appropriating this amulet in the decades that separate us, the tribesmen down in the village believe – quite rightly – that, by entering the Temple of the Great Being Marram-ap, they will release a swarm of Vespa mandarinina, *the giant Asian hornet.*

Although aware of the fact that, like all males of our line, you will most likely be immune to their sting, I would imagine that encountering the swarm would be exceedingly unpleasant.

By the time you have spent a little time regarding the artwork between here and the door, opened this cylindrical container and read thus far, the hornets will have woken from their slumber.

So, grasp the letter, and run like the wind!

Affectionately yours,
Hannibal

Will's ears filled with the sound of insect wings. Not a drowsy summer meadow bumble-bee buzzing, but a ferocious orchestra of raw terror.

He swivelled round.

Careering at him from all directions were tens of thousands of giant hornets, the size of golf balls. The temple was filled with them.

Overcome with a sense of panic, Will tossed the cylinder to the floor, grabbed the letter, and fled.

From *Hannibal Fogg and the Supreme Secret of Man*

The Angry Mountain

At La Planète, the huddle of legs began to untangle themselves and their owners attempted uneasily to stand. Zak pulled up the boy – who was about nine and had a terrible hangover. His name was Marcus.

'Well guys,' began Zak in a drawl, 'thanks for the floor space, that was a rad night. D'you have plans today?'

'Yes,' I said, 'we're off to climb the Nyiragongo volcano – the angry mountain. It's a very special, international scientific expedition.'

Oswaldo had been leaping about since he had heard about the Nyiragongo and its significance: he loved volcanoes.

'Che!' he cried out. 'Can Zake came claymeng vocannow? Pleeese che.'

I muttered that Zak and Marcus could tag along if they would aid the expedition in every way possible. They promised to do so.

Marcus grabbed up the chicken. We left La Planète and started out of Goma, hoping for a truck to pick us up. Oswaldo and I were laden with our belongings. I would always keep my saddle-bags nearby, even though at times they could be inconvenient. Various hardened travellers had cautioned me never to leave my possessions alone for a moment in Africa. I noticed that they generally travelled by car. Some had porters to carry the baggage. None had ancient saddle-bags.

A massive sculpted hand – clutching a burning torch – sprang forth from a triangle of white cement like Excalibur: the symbol of Mobutu's tyranny. We tiptoed past.

The Nyiragongo volcano had apparently last erupted in 1977, sending a three-metre-high wall of lava towards Goma and forcing the townspeople to flee into Rwanda. Oswaldo spluttered all he knew about erupting volcanoes: he had once done a school project on Parangaricutiro, a village covered by the erupting lava of the Paricutin volcano in Mexico.

Marcus was a peculiar boy: he chain-smoked lumps of black tobacco which he rolled in broad green leaves. He never said anything, just ambled along behind the rest of us, pulling at the string to make his chicken hurry. I asked Zak if Marcus spoke English. He replied:

'Man, he don't speak nothin'. He was hexed as a baby... best dude I ever knew.'

I wondered how Zak had found out that Marcus had been bewitched, if they were unable to communicate in speech: indeed, how did anyone know to call him Marcus? But it would have been rude, somehow, to have asked.

Zak, who came from Seattle, had played ice hockey for Washington State. His body was muscular and stocky, and his feet were size thirteen: perfect for the world of professional ice hockey. Zak had a set of crude false teeth – many of his own teeth had been knocked out in hockey matches. He would remove the dentures from time to time and put them in his jeans pocket. 'They're a bit too big,' he mumbled, as he carried on chatting. His stories of players having fingers sliced off with skates and limbs gashed made Oswaldo and me reel in abhorrence.

'Zak, what exactly brought you to Zaire?' I asked, for it seemed curious that an ice hockey star should be attracted to Central Africa.

'Well,' he said slowly, 'there is a reason.'

'What is it?' I probed inquisitively.

'*Mokele-Mbembe*,' he said.

'What on earth is that?'

'It's supposed to exist in the most remote parts of the jungle, where it lives in caves and on the banks of rivers.'

'But *what* exactly is it like?'

'Its body is said to be as large as an elephant's; some say it has a giant horn mounted on its nose; its neck is long and muscular, and the tail is like that of an alligator. It can live on the land or in water, and it's a kinda greyish-brown colour and about thirty feet long.'

'Deenosaw!' said Oswaldo firmly, wiggling about.

'Yeah man, it's a kinda dinosaur. I came here to track it. No one from the West has ever positively seen one. I figured if I hung out here long enough I'd eventually bump into a specimen.'

'Searching for Mokele has not been easy,' said Zak pensively.

'Why soo hard, amigo?' asked the Patagonian.

'Well,' said Zak candidly, 'there's an old pygmy myth which makes things a bit tricky.'

'What do the pygmies say?' I inquired.

'They say that if you see Mokele-Mbembe and

tell of it, you will die a horrible and agonizing death... so getting witnesses to step forward has been hindered.'

'Is this the precise area it's supposed to be living?' I asked.

'Not exactly,' began Zak, 'it's thought to exist mainly around the Mainyu river over in Cameroon.'

'Did you go and look over there already?'

'Yup.'

'How long did you stick it out?'

'Eighteen months,' said Zak. 'I guess we just never bumped into each other over there... so I came to this part of the jungle. I like it here.'

Maybe, I mused, Zak had seen the legendary creature already, but was gagged by the peril of the pygmy myth.

After we had walked for an hour, a petrol tanker rolled along. Zak jumped into the road and the driver slammed on the brakes.

'Yo man, we need to go to the Nyiragongo! You dig?'

The African driver, who was recovering from the whiplash of the emergency stop, threw up his arms and said, '*Quoi?*'

'Hey man I don't speak ya language, you speak American?'

The driver spat. Oswaldo blushed and asked in his own brand of French if the vehicle was going towards the Nyiragongo. It was. Although Zak had spent such a long time searching for the mysterious Mokele-Mbembe, he had not mastered any Central African dialects, let alone French. The driver motioned us to climb aboard. We jumped up onto the slippery tanker and clung on as it squirmed between deep potholes towards our goal. Near to Kibati, on the Rutshuru Road, we descended.

Out of the jungle undergrowth rose the steep slopes of the Nyiragongo. A sense of primeval desertion surrounded the remote peak: this was the very centre of Gondwanaland.

As we stood in awe and breathed in deeply, I could taste the sulphur and vapours on my tongue. A silence, the like of which I had never before known, surrounded us. Everything was still, almost as if in respect for this quintessential form. Torrential rain began to pour from the sky. Yet, instead of taking cover, we all stood in wonder and felt strangely affected.

A boy wearing purple plastic shoes appeared from nowhere, a banana leaf shading his head. He could take us to the top for a few *zaires*. Oswaldo handed him a note and he led the way. As we climbed higher up the thin mud path, the terrain changed in density to a lighter mixture of ferns and shrubs. Marcus choked now and then and exhaled black smoke in time with his steps. Steam sprang from fissures on either side of the track. And the stench of sulphur was all around.

After about five hours of climbing we reached the cloud level. It was like walking into a wet, white sheet. Zak sang hockey songs, with Oswaldo improvising, as the child in purple plastic slippers leapt from crag to crag ahead of the group. He turned to Marcus and asked him a question in Lingala. Marcus said nothing, as usual, but looked at the sky and put his left hand on the back of his neck. The other boy nodded. Whenever anyone asked Marcus a question, whether in Lingala or French, he did this. It seemed to make perfect sense to all Zairean people.

The enormous chicken squawked and stopped to peck at the mud. I wondered if it was the first domestic fowl ever to have ascended the Nyiragongo.

By the time we reached the layer of solidified lava, Zak was staggering along with Oswaldo stretched across his arms. There was still no sign of the Gonds' sister tribe. Oswaldo moaned in Spanish the words from 'La Cucaracha' that there was no way he could walk another step. The boy in purple plastic shoes looked round, surprise on his face that we could have been afflicted so easily with such exhaustion.

Suddenly, a bushy red beard pushed out of the apparently virgin undergrowth. It was attached to the face of a massive Australian. He had ferns tied to his feet and was carrying a banana leaf on his head. His name, he informed us, was Howard.

'G'day sport! What's new from the old country?' he asked me.

I replied that as far as I knew everything was fine. Pulling a bottle of Primus lager from his belt, he bit off the top, and indicated that it should be passed around. Marcus' eyes lit up. He snatched the brown glass bottle and gulped down the contents in five seconds flat. Howard looked sad that a minor should have already taken such a liking to drink. I asked Howard what he was doing in Zaire.

'Well, things in Brisbane were down, really down. Felt it was time to chuck in the job and go walkabout.'

'What did you do in Australia?' I asked.

'I was a computer systems analyst.' He chuckled.

There was something I had to know. Plucking up courage, I put the question bluntly, 'Howard, please tell me why you're wearing ferns on your feet and a banana leaf on your head.'

He looked at me as if I was absolutely insane: as if I were enquiring why birds fly. He shook his head slowly and said, 'Don't you know?'

Then he walked off into the undergrowth again.

Zaire had a strange quality which, however unpleasant the conditions, made it assuredly one of the most enchanted places. Completely unexpected things would happen. I had been guilty of thinking like a Westerner when challenging the reasons for Howard's appearance. The Australian had striven to cast away these obstacles of thought – leaving behind the life and mentality of a systems analyst – to attain salvation in the Zairean rain forest.

The longer I stayed in Zaire, the more outlandish seemed the events which took place, and the more I began to understand the limitations of my knowledge of people. Real people.

The boy in purple plastic shoes shouted out. We had reached the crater. There was no one about. Perhaps Jacques had been mistakenly informed about the Gonds' sister tribe; but what faced me now drove all thoughts of lost peoples from my mind.

I had expected the crater to be a few feet wide: nothing serious, just a gap. Rain plunged down as we sat on the rim, and stared in stupefaction at its enormousness. The Nyiragongo's diameter seemed to be several hundred metres across. Black cloud was mixed with the steam that bathed us. Oswaldo yelled louder than I had heard him yell before. No echo followed his roar and, in a remarkable way, his cries hardly dented the silence.

As he held my legs, I bent over the precipice.

Exhilaration and a sense of absolute elation grasped me, as I peered down through an abyss of vapour. The Nyiragongo was alive – I was sure of it – and I could almost sense it breathing. Was this not Gondwanaland's core pulsing beneath me?

Our guide was growing nervous. It would soon be night and we should descend the volcano before darkness fell. Noises of the twilight had begun in the rain forest, as wild animals caught their evening prey and birds sang out in warning of our presence.

Oswaldo, Zak, Marcus, the chicken and I reached the road and started to walk towards Goma. An hour later there was still no sign of a car. At ten pm, the whine of an engine was heard, then headlights appeared, and a small white Renault came to a halt just in front of us. The driver was Belgian. A doctor – going to a patient in a village halfway to Goma – he was willing to take us to the crossroads where he had to turn off.

The old settler chatted away in excellent English about the days before African rule.

'I remember when there was a dying man

at the top of the Nyiragongo,' he said. 'I had to climb up at night to save him. There was so much snow that we built an igloo on the summit to take shelter, as we couldn't move the patient for three days until more painkillers came.'

The doctor had been unable to re-adjust to his native country after living in Central Africa for so many years. I was beginning to understand the curious, addictive force of Africa. The longer one stayed, the more dependent upon it one became.

At the crossroads we clambered out of the car. It hooted twice and drove away, leaving us in the middle of nowhere. Oswaldo switched on the penlight torch he always carried in case of an emergency. We walked for hours. Morale plummeted. Zak's ice-hockey jokes had been told and told again, and a steady stream of rain fell from the night sky. After a few miles we saw a side road that seemed as if it might lead off to a village.

By group decision we agreed to take a chance and venture down the track. Several miles later the road suddenly ran out, and a wall of jungle sprang from the ground in front. Maybe the track had been reclaimed by the jungle, or perhaps never finished. The rain fell harder and we assembled in a huddle. Marcus grasped the bedraggled chicken close to his chest for warmth and we each moaned in turn.

But in Zaire, when things were at their lowest ebb, something unusual always happened.

A pretty teenage girl stepped out of the jungle ahead of us. I wondered for a moment if she was from the Gonds' sister tribe, but she did not resemble the Indian Gonds. Her hair was twined in hundreds of short antennae and her cheeks had dimples. We followed her into the undergrowth. It seemed as if we were entering an enchanted forest: each of us stepped cautiously with expectation.

The trees sprouted taller and thicker, and the stars were hidden by their foliage. After an hour or so of trudging I began to fear a trap. Something or other, at any rate, was going to befall us.

Suddenly, Oswaldo stopped whining and stood motionless. Then Zak and Marcus froze, transfixed. I stared up at one of the most phenomenal sights I had ever seen: a château of typical European design stood squarely in front of us. Its reflection was visible, lit by the moon, in Lake Kivu.

The girl shuffled towards it and we followed, each of us thunderstruck.

A figure, bent over with age, moved towards us in the darkness. He looked even more shocked than we to meet like this. Addressing me in French, in an almost poetic tone, he said:

'You have returned! We have waited all these years. I knew that this night would come.'

Moving over to Zak, he hugged him with all the strength left in his frail arms. His wife – who was much younger – walked over, her eyes peering to focus on us. She put out her fingers to touch mine. The door of the château was unlocked with a great iron key and pushed open. As I tried to come to terms with the paradoxical circumstances of the night, we entered the building, guided by Oswaldo's penlight.

From *Beyond the Devil's Teeth*

A Request

If you enjoyed this book, please review it on Amazon and Goodreads.

Reviews are an author's best friend.

To stay in touch with Tahir Shah, and to hear about his upcoming releases before anyone else, please sign up for his mailing list:

 http://tahirshah.com/newsletter

And to follow him on social media, please go to any of the following links:

 http://www.twitter.com/humanstew

 http://www.facebook.com/TahirShahAuthor

 http://www.youtube.com/user/tahirshah999

 http://www.pinterest.com/tahirshah

 http://tahirshah.com/goodreads

 https://www.instagram.com/Tahirshah999/

http://www.tahirshah.com

Made in the USA
Las Vegas, NV
14 June 2021

24744149R00109